Common Core Progress Monitor™

English Language Arts

Sadlier School

Copyright © by William H. Sadlier, Inc. All rights reserved.

Contents

Cover: *Series Design:* Studio Montage; *Title Design:* Quarasan, Inc.

Interior Photo: Hermann Krone: 11.

For additional online resources, go to SadlierConnect.com.

Copyright © 2014 by William H. Sadlier, Inc. All rights reserved.

This publication, or any part thereof, may not be reproduced in any form, or by any means, including electronic, photographic, or mechanical, or by any sound recording system, or by any device for storage or retrieval of information, without the written permission of the publisher. Address inquiries to Permission Department, William H. Sadlier, Inc., 9 Pine Street, New York, NY 10005-4700.

S® is a registered trademark of William H. Sadlier, Inc.

William H. Sadlier, Inc.
9 Pine Street
New York, NY 10005-4700

Printed in the United States of America.
ISBN: 978-1-4217-3073-8
2 3 4 5 6 7 8 9 C 17 16 15 14

Common Core State Standards Copyright © 2010. National Governors Association Center for Best Practices and Council of Chief State School Officers. All rights reserved.

Read the passage. Then answer the questions.

Snow White and Rose Red

1 Snow White and Rose Red were sisters. They lived with their mother in a cabin in the countryside. Rose Red liked to run through meadows and catch butterflies. Snow White liked to stay close to home. Even though they were different, Snow White and Rose Red were best friends. They always held hands and promised to never leave each other.

2 One cold winter night, with the wind howling like a wolf, someone knocked on the door. Thinking it was a traveler, the girls' mother opened the door. A large black bear stood in the doorway. The bear said he meant no harm. The mother invited the bear inside to get warm. Snow White and Rose Red brushed the snow from the bear's fur. He stretched out in front of the fire. The girls played games with him. He growled playfully.

3 The bear came back to the cabin every night. The bear, the girls, and the mother all became good friends. Winter turned to spring and then to summer. The bear told them that someone wanted to steal his riches. The bear needed to guard his treasures, which had been frozen underground. Snow White and Rose Red were sad to see him go.

4 Soon after, Snow White and Rose Red went into the forest for firewood. They found a little man whose beard was stuck in tree branches. As the girls tried to free him, he called them names. The sisters still wanted to help. Finally, Snow White used scissors to cut off the end of the beard. The man shouted, "You ruined my beautiful beard!"

5 Later, as Snow White and Rose Red walked by a pond, they saw the little man again. This time, he was fishing. A large fish on the end of the line was pulling him toward the water. The girls grabbed his arms to save him, and he dropped the fishing rod. "That was my dinner!" he yelled as he stomped away.

Copyright © by William H. Sadlier, Inc. All rights reserved.

6 One afternoon, the sisters heard someone scream. An eagle was lifting the little man off the ground to take him to its nest! The girls rushed to his aid and convinced the bird to let go. After Snow White and Rose Red saved the little man for the third time, he screamed, "Stop it! Stop!"

7 Suddenly, the little man disappeared into thin air! As the girls wondered what happened, a handsome man with black hair approached them. "Don't you know me?" he asked. It was the bear! The little man had cursed this prince by turning him into a bear when he refused to hand over his riches. The kindness of the sisters forced the little man to vanish, lifting the curse.

8 The prince was very grateful to Snow White and Rose Red. He shared his treasures with them and made them both queens. The sisters lived close to each other for the rest of their lives, keeping their promise to stay together forever.

1. Which sentences below best describe the central message of this fairy tale?

I Talking bears are good friends.

II Being kind and helpful is better than being mean.

III Fishing can be dangerous.

IV Working together is important.

A Items I and III are correct.

B Items II and III are correct.

C Items II and IV are correct.

D Items III and IV are correct.

2. **Part A** Which word best describes the little man?

A nice

B mean

C afraid

D tricky

Part B Which paragraph from the story best supports the answer to Part A?

A paragraph 1

B paragraph 2

C paragraph 3

D paragraph 4

Copyright © by William H. Sadlier, Inc. All rights reserved.

3. Part A Reread paragraph 2. What does ***the wind howling like a wolf*** mean?

A A wolf is howling outside the cabin.

B The wind is so loud that it makes a knocking sound on the door.

C Wind is strongest in the wintertime.

D The wind was loud and frightening.

Part B What other detail in the paragraph best supports the answer to Part A?

A "One cold winter night"

B "someone knocked on the door"

C "He stretched out in front of the fire."

D "He growled playfully."

4. Part A Why does the prince share his treasures with Snow White and Rose Red?

A He wanted to ask Snow White to marry him.

B He wanted to reward them for their kindness and for breaking the curse.

C He had to share his treasures to break the curse.

D He did not want to share them with the little man.

Part B Which sentence from the story best supports the answer to Part A?

A "The kindness of the sisters forced the little man to vanish, lifting the curse."

B "The bear needed to guard his treasures, which had been frozen underground."

C "The bear, the girls, and the mother all became good friends."

D "Even though they were different, Snow White and Rose Red were best friends."

5. Reread paragraph 7 of the story. What does ***vanish*** mean?

A disappear

B wonder

C approach

D kindness

Copyright © by William H. Sadlier, Inc. All rights reserved.

Read the passage. Then answer the questions.

Zora Neale Hurston

(1891–1960)

1 Zora Neale Hurston began her career during the Harlem Renaissance. This movement celebrated African American artists and writers of the 1920s. As a confident and friendly young woman, Hurston fit perfectly into this cultural celebration.

2 Hurston spent her childhood in African American communities throughout the South. One left a lasting impression on her. It was Eatonville, Florida, the oldest all–African American town. There, African Americans ran the government. They taught in the schools. They owned all the businesses. In this community, Hurston took pride in herself and in her African American heritage.

3 During the Harlem Renaissance, many wealthy New Yorkers gave money to support artists and writers. These people were called patrons. Hurston easily found a patron for her research. With that money, Hurston used what she learned in college to study different African American communities. She traveled all around the South. She also traveled through Haiti and Jamaica.

4 Hurston collected African American folktales during her trips. Characters like the smart rabbit and the hero Jack moved in and out of these stories. The stories changed depending on who told them. No matter what version it was, the folktale always sparked the imaginations of anyone who would listen.

5 Hurston wrote these tales down in collections. She also used her memories of Eatonville to write her own stories. One, "John Redding Goes to Sea," tells of a boy who wishes to go "to where the sky touches the ground." Hurston's stories were filled with characters like John. Her characters had big dreams and interesting stories to tell. She wrote their stories using the words her characters might use if they were real people. You can almost hear the characters telling their own stories.

Copyright © by William H. Sadlier, Inc. All rights reserved.

6 As her career went on, people stopped reading Hurston's stories. Some people thought she should write about race issues or politics, not about everyday life in the rural South. Soon those people's opinions took over. By Hurston's death in 1960, publishers had stopped printing her books.

7 However, public opinion did not stay the same. Other African American writers found Hurston's work. They recognized the value and beauty in her stories. They wanted to read about regular people. Since this rediscovery, Hurston has been considered one of the best writers of her time. Hurston's collections and fiction continue to thrill readers, just like the African American folktales that inspired her stories.

6. **Part A** What does ***patron*** mean in paragraph 3?

A a person from Harlem who creates art

B a rich person who supports an artist or writer

C a person who buys and sells art

D a person who starts an artistic movement

Part B Which statement from the passage best explains how Hurston used the money from her patron?

A "These people were called patrons."

B "Hurston easily found a patron for her research."

C "With that money, Hurston used what she learned in college to study different African American communities."

D "They taught in the schools."

7. Which of the following statements describes how the sentences in paragraph 4 are related?

A The paragraph compares the folktales Hurston collected in the South to folktales people told in the North.

B The paragraph describes what causes Hurston to write down the folktales and explains the effects of recording them.

C The paragraph describes the steps Hurston took to record the folktales she heard in the South.

D The first sentence indicates the topic, folktales, and the other sentences give more details about the topic.

Copyright © by William H. Sadlier, Inc. All rights reserved.

8. **Part A** Which key words would you use to search for more about Hurston's research and writing?

I folktales

II patron

III American

IV heritage

V Hurston

A Items I and III are correct.

B Items I and V are correct.

C Items II, IV, and V are correct.

D Items III and V are correct.

Part B Which of the following statements from the passage would you most likely find by using the search terms in Part A?

A "Zora Neale Hurston began her career during the Harlem Renaissance."

B "Hurston took pride in herself and in her African American heritage."

C "Hurston collected African American folktales during her trips."

D "Other African American writers found Hurston's work."

9. **Part A** Based on the information in the passage, what phrase best describes the Harlem Renaissance?

A a movement that supported African American artists and writers

B a movement that connected patrons to deserving artists and writers

C a place in New York City where artists and writers shared ideas

D a group of artists and writers who gathered and performed African American folktales

Part B Which statement from the passage best describes Hurston's relationship to the Harlem Renaissance?

A "Hurston spent her childhood in African American communities throughout the South."

B "As a confident and friendly young woman, Hurston fit perfectly into this cultural celebration."

C "During the Harlem Renaissance, many wealthy New Yorkers gave money to support artists and writers."

D "She traveled all around the South. She also traveled through Haiti and Jamaica."

Copyright © by William H. Sadlier, Inc. All rights reserved.

Read the passage. Then answer the questions.

The Trilobite Trip

1 Kyle was extremely frustrated. All he wanted to do before leaving New Mexico was to find a few fossils. He had been such a good sport for the whole trip. Now he was about to miss his last chance.

2 It was the last day of his parents' artist residence in Taos. They were painters. So that they could work in peace, Kyle and his sister Lulu went to day camp. Kyle thought it was fine. They could swim, canoe, and learn Native American crafts. Activities did not include hiking, though, and Kyle needed to get into the hills to look for fossils.

3 Scientists use fossils to learn the history of Earth. At home, Kyle had been painting a map onto an old Ping-Pong table. It showed the location of fossils in North America. Kyle met a fossil expert while waiting in a line one day, and it changed his life. As a result, Kyle learned about trilobites. Hundreds of kinds of buglike trilobites lived when oceans covered the land. Their fossils showed up from New York to New Mexico, Utah, and beyond. Tracing trilobites became Kyle's mission.

4 Today his parents had signed the family up for a balloon ride. Kyle's plan was to act really, really scared so that his parents would leave him behind. His acting was not working, though. His mother kept telling him he would love the ride. Lulu made fun of him for being scared. His father just laughed. Kyle gave up his plan and got into the basket of the balloon.

5 Up they went. It was really pretty nice. The basket of the balloon did not sway. Looking out was like watching a movie. With a small ache in his heart, Kyle gazed at the hills he should be climbing right now to find trilobites.

6 A gust of wind shifted the balloon. The pilot said they would have to land soon. The chase car far below them was already hunting for a road to take to meet the balloon.

Copyright © by William H. Sadlier, Inc. All rights reserved.

7 The pilot found a field to land in, but it was far from the nearest road. When they landed, the pilot jumped out to tie them down and let the air out of the balloon. He radioed the chase car. It was still far away. There were farm buildings in the distance.

8 Kyle considered the situation. He was still aching to look for fossils, and maybe he would have time while they waited for the car, so he volunteered to meet the car at the farm. The pilot looked at his parents. They nodded. Off Kyle ran.

9 As he got closer to the farmhouse, the field gave way to gravel. Because he was looking at the rocks, Kyle did not see the boulder until after he tripped. There, next to his hand as he pushed up to keep going, was a trilobite fossil. Yes! The trip was a success after all.

10. What is the central message of the "The Trilobite Trip"?

A Everyone should study fossils.

B Focusing on one thing for too long takes the fun out of life.

C Good luck needs to be supported by preparation.

D Some projects are impossible.

11. **Part A** Which event from the story made Kyle want to learn about trilobites?

A Kyle met a fossil expert.

B Kyle found a boulder.

C Kyle and his family took a balloon ride.

D Kyle and his sister went to day camp.

Part B Which phrase from the story is related to the event in Part A?

A "before leaving New Mexico"

B "while waiting in a line one day"

C "use fossils to learn the history of Earth"

D "as he pushed up to keep going"

12. In paragraph 3, what does ***mission*** mean?

A occasional hobby

B biggest challenge

C dream

D main purpose

Copyright © by William H. Sadlier, Inc. All rights reserved.

Read the passage. Then answer the questions.

How Fossils Form

1 Imagine yourself in your hometown millions of years ago. Would you be underwater or on land? What would the plants look like? What types of animals would you see? Today, scientists gather clues left behind by ancient living things to answer these questions.

2 Fossils, or the remains of ancient living things, come in many shapes and sizes. There are two main groups of fossils: body fossils and trace fossils. A body fossil actually shows part of the animal or plant itself. A trace fossil is a record of something the animal or plant did or made. A trace fossil might be a footprint or the impression of a leaf. Fossils help scientists figure out how ancient animals and plants looked and behaved. They also help show how the environment has changed over time. Scientists find and study fossils to put together a story of the Earth long ago.

3 Where does a fossil form? Fossils usually form in sediment. Sediment can be bits of sand, clay, or soil. This sediment builds up in layers. Over time, the layers get pressed together, forming sedimentary rock. The walls of the Grand Canyon are examples of sedimentary rock. Scientists find most fossils in sedimentary rock.

Fossil from the Saxonian Cretaceous basin of impressions made by an ancient animal similar to shrimp and lobsters

4 A trace fossil can start with a simple footprint. Imagine a *Tyrannosaurus rex* stomping through the soil millions of years ago. It makes prints in the ground. Each print hardens and dries. Then it is covered with sediment. Over time, more and more sediment covers the print, burying it under layers of rock.

Copyright © by William H. Sadlier, Inc. All rights reserved.

5 Other trace fossils form when a leaf or other living thing is pressed into sediment. As the living thing decomposes, it leaves a print. The living thing is gone, but now the sediment has an impression that looks just like it!

6 The soft parts of a living thing usually do not form a fossil. However, the hard parts of animals, like bones, teeth, and shells, can form body fossils. First, the hard body part is buried in sediment. Over time, the bone, tooth, or shell is replaced with minerals. These minerals take the same shape as the bone, tooth, or shell, but are hard and heavy.

7 Fossils are not the only way scientists can learn about insects and plants. Sometimes, whole insects and plants get trapped in tree sap. They get stuck, nearly unchanged, for millions of years! Even animals as large as mammoths have been preserved. These large animals were frozen in large sheets of ice, where they remained until scientists discovered them thousands of years later.

13. Which statement best describes the main idea of "How Fossils Form"?

A Sedimentary rock is formed over a long period of time.

B Scientists study fossils to learn about the past.

C North America looked different millions of years ago.

D Some body fossils are formed by buried bones.

14. **Part A** Which shows the correct order of steps for how a trace fossil forms?

I Sediment covers the print.

II An animal steps in soft soil.

III The print hardens and dries.

IV Layers of rock bury the print.

A I, II, IV, III

B II, I, III, IV

C II, III, I, IV

D II, IV, I, III

Part B Which detail in the passage tells you the first step in the formation of a trace fossil?

A "A trace fossil is a record of something the animal or plant did or made."

B "First, the hard body part is buried in sediment."

C "A trace fossil can start with a simple footprint."

D "As the living thing decomposes, it leaves a print."

Copyright © by William H. Sadlier, Inc. All rights reserved.

15. Which type of fossil is shown in the image?

A a trace fossil

B a shrimp fossil

C a preserved fossil

D a Saxonian fossil

16. Based on key details in "The Trilobite Trip" and "How Fossils Form," which of the following statements is most likely true?

A Kyle found the trilobite fossil in a piece of sedimentary rock.

B It would be easy to find a trace fossil of a trilobite.

C Sedimentary rock is rare in the United States.

D Kyle's map will help explain the history of people in the United States.

17. Based on details in "The Trilobite Trip" and "How Fossils Form," how can scientists know that trilobites were "buglike"?

A Trilobites crept along the ocean floor like bugs.

B Trilobites were preserved in tree sap.

C Trilobite fossils appear in many parts of the United States, and so do bugs.

D Trilobites formed body fossils.

18. Which statements are based on points from "The Trilobite Trip" and "How Fossils Form"?

I Over time, the environment of North America has changed.

II The path a chase car follows could become a trace fossil.

III Hunting for and studying fossils is a branch of science.

IV Showing the location of trilobites can reveal some of Earth's past.

A Items I and II are correct.

B Items II and III are correct.

C Items I, III, and IV are correct.

D Items II, III, and IV are correct.

Copyright © by William H. Sadlier, Inc. All rights reserved.

Read the passage. Then answer the questions.

True Heroes

True heroes are the fine folks who
Take time to lend a hand.
They're the people who speak out,
Who take risks and make a stand.

Firefighters put their lives at risk
To quench a fiery blaze.
They bash down doors and smash through walls
To search for lives to save.

A doctor smooths a plaster cast
Around a fractured arm.
The doctor treats the splintered bone.
And keeps it safe from harm.

Volunteers bring meals to people's homes
And take shelter dogs for walks.
Some volunteers call on the sick
To help, to listen, to talk.

Let heroes' deeds inspire you
To help, to listen, to care.
There are many ways to be a hero
You just need to be aware.

Copyright © by William H. Sadlier, Inc. All rights reserved.

Go on

19. Which stanzas of the poem best support the idea that being a hero can involve taking care of living things?

A stanzas 1, 2, and 3

B stanzas 2, 3, and 4

C stanzas 3, 4, and 5

D stanzas 1, 3, and 5

20. **Part A** Read lines 1–2 from the poem. What does ***to lend a hand*** most likely mean?

A to help someone with a task

B to help someone push an object

C to lift an object with one hand

D to offer a handshake

Part B Which line from the poem is not an example of someone "lending a hand"?

A "They're the people who speak out"

B "They bash down doors and smash through walls"

C "There are many ways to be a hero"

D "Volunteers bring meals to people's homes"

21. Which of the following best defines ***fractured*** in stanza 3 of the poem?

A flattened

B healed

C protected

D broken

Copyright © by William H. Sadlier, Inc. All rights reserved.

22. Based on the poem, draw a line from each item in the Central Message or Key Detail column to the related examples in the Example column. Note that the poem has only one central message.

Central Message or Key Detail	**Example**
1 Central Message	**a** Helping heal injuries
2 Key Detail	**b** Visiting people who are sick
	c Standing up for what is right
	d Everyone can be a hero.
	e Taking care of animals

23. Based on the poem, draw a line from each item in the Stanza column to an item in the Example column to show which stanza includes which example.

Stanza	**Example**
1 Stanza 1	**a** Recognizing ways to help
2 Stanza 2	**b** Taking a chance
3 Stanza 3	**c** Bringing food to people
4 Stanza 4	**d** Putting out fires
5 Stanza 5	**e** Treating an injury

Copyright © by William H. Sadlier, Inc. All rights reserved.

Stop

Read the passage. Then answer the questions.

New Friends

1 Raz felt nervous. She looked down at her pencil case and backpack on the floor between her feet. She looked up at the faces of the girls and boys she had not met yet. It was her first morning at this school, even though it was December. Raz's family had just moved to town, and Raz was going to finish the year here at Washington School.

2 The teacher introduced Raz to the class, telling them her name and the name of the school she had attended for the first half of the year. "It can be hard to make a big change in the middle of the school year. Let's do everything we can to make Raz feel welcome!" the teacher said to the class.

3 Maria watched Raz sit down at an empty desk. Maria had transferred to Washington School last year. She knew what it was like to start over with new classmates. Maria loved math and could not wait for the science fair each year. She quickly made friends with other kids in her class. They shared their excitement about math and science.

4 Pete also looked at the new girl. He remembered what it was like to be new to school. Pete was a huge sports fan. He played at least one sport every season of the year. He joined teams at school. Pete made friends who loved sports as much as he did.

5 Other than moving to the same town at the same time, Maria and Pete did not have much in common. They had started at Washington School on the same day, but they did not play or eat their lunches together.

6 Later that day, Maria asked Raz about the stickers on her pencil case. There were horses, brightly colored fish, and other animals. "I like horses, and I like tropical fish," Maria said. "What are the other animals on your stickers?" she asked.

7 Raz and Maria talked about the other stickers. There were jaguars, beavers, and otters. There were also tigers, giraffes, and whales. Pete heard them talking and came over to join them. Pete told Raz that he

Copyright © by William H. Sadlier, Inc. All rights reserved.

liked the patches on her backpack. "I know some of the team logos, but not all of them. Where are they all from? Which one is your favorite soccer team?" he asked.

8 Maria, Raz, and Pete kept talking. Pete said that he was looking forward to spring, when he could play baseball and volleyball. Raz told them that at her old school, she had played volleyball and soccer. Maria mentioned that the science fair this year would be in the spring and that she was excited about it. Pete rolled his eyes and looked at Raz.

9 "That's great," said Raz. "I love the science fair, too. Maybe we can all work together on a project!" Smiles broke out on the children's faces. Pete and Maria both nodded. They had never thought that they would be friends. Raz had shown them that you do not have to like all the same things to get along.

24. Which description of Raz does evidence in the passage support?

A Raz's favorite subject is math.

B Raz likes only soccer and volleyball.

C Raz has always attended Washington School.

D Raz enjoys science and sports.

25. What does this sentence from paragraph 4 most likely mean?

"Pete was a huge sports fan."

A Pete is very tall.

B Pete likes sports very much.

C Pete likes sports that are hugely popular.

D Pete does not like sports.

26. Which sentence from the story describes Pete's character?

A "It was her first morning at this school, even though it was December."

B "Pete made friends who loved sports as much as he did."

C "Pete also looked at the new girl."

D "Pete heard them talking and came over to join them."

27. What does this sentence from paragraph 9 most likely mean?

"Smiles broke out on the children's faces."

A The children smiled politely.

B The children began to frown.

C The children smiled.

D Smiles left the children's faces.

Copyright © by William H. Sadlier, Inc. All rights reserved.

28. Write numbers 1–5 on the lines to put the scenes from the story in order, from the first event (1) to the last event (5).

_____ Raz arrives at Washington School.

_____ Maria and Raz talk about Raz's animal stickers.

_____ Maria and Pete start at Washington School.

_____ Raz suggests that all three work on a science project.

_____ Pete asks Raz a question about sports.

29. What point of view is the story told from: a narrator or a character in the story? How is it different from your own point of view?

____

____

____

____

____

____

____

____

Copyright © by William H. Sadlier, Inc. All rights reserved.

30. In your opinion, what is the most important message of the story? Give one reason to support your opinion. Use details from at least two paragraphs of the story to support your reason. Identify the paragraph where you found each detail.

Copyright © by William H. Sadlier, Inc. All rights reserved.

Planning Page

You may use this space to plan your writing for question 31. Do NOT write your final answer to question 31 on this page. The notes on this page will NOT count as part of your answer to question 31.

Copyright © by William H. Sadlier, Inc. All rights reserved.

31. What do Maria and Pete have in common? What does this lead them to do? Describe how their actions and words at the end of the story build on what the teacher says in paragraph 2. Use at least three details from the passage to support your answer.

In your response, be sure to:

- ☐ Introduce the characters and their similarities.
- ☐ Describe how the characters' similarities influence their actions and build on the teacher's comments.
- ☐ Use details from the passage to develop your ideas.
- ☐ Connect your ideas with linking words and phrases.
- ☐ End with a concluding statement.

Copyright © by William H. Sadlier, Inc. All rights reserved.

Copyright © by William H. Sadlier, Inc. All rights reserved.

Stop

Read the passage. Then answer the questions.

Two Worlds, Different but Alike

1 March 3, 2013

Dear Emilia,

2 Tell me all about your life in Mexico! I live in Bayside, Queens. Queens is one of the five boroughs of New York City in the state of New York. My family lives in an apartment. I have my own bedroom. My brothers Ari and Ben share a room.

3 Our school year is from September through June. The school day starts at 8:30 in the morning. It ends at 2:50 in the afternoon. We get one half-hour for lunch, and we also get recess. At recess we can play or take an activity. I study violin. I love music. My favorite subjects are math and music. I hope to be in an orchestra some day. What are your town and school like?

4 Your friend,

5 Abby

6 March 29, 2013

Dear Abby,

7 I, too, am excited to have a pen pal! My family and I live on a farm. It is just outside of the town of Villanueva in the state of Zacatecas. We also go to school from September through June. School starts at 9 o'clock in the morning. It ends at 3 o'clock. I like school and hope one day to become a doctor. My favorite subjects are mathematics and art. I study English on Saturdays.

8 When we come home from school, we help our mother in the house or our father on the farm. We raise cattle, but we also raise vegetables to sell in town on weekends. That is very exciting. I love watching all of the people in the plaza. Tell me what it is like to live in a large city.

9 Your friend,

10 Emilia

Go on

Copyright © by William H. Sadlier, Inc. All rights reserved.

11 April 24, 2013

Dear Emilia,

12 Living in a large city with all of the people is fun, but sometimes people need help. When my father was 21, he decided to become a firefighter. Being a New York City firefighter isn't easy. Sometimes Dad has to fight fires in very large buildings and help people get out of the buildings. There are also times when we have really bad storms. My father and other firefighters help people get out of the path of the storm or out of flooded areas. My father never thinks about himself. He just works hard for everybody else. He is my hero. Who is your hero, Emilia?

13 Your friend,

14 Abby

15 May 16, 2013

Dear Abby,

16 Your dad sounds like a great person. My heroes are my grandparents. They started our farm. They had to work long hours by themselves to make it successful. There were years when they had few vegetables to sell, so they made the decision to raise cattle. It was not easy, but they did it. I admire my grandparents for working so hard. They hired other people to work on our farm. The farm is now successful. My father runs it, but my grandparents still help. I love watching them work and smile at each other. They are my heroes! Write back. Tell me about playing the violin.

17 Your friend,

18 Emilia

Copyright © by William H. Sadlier, Inc. All rights reserved.

32. From which character's point of view is paragraph 2 written? From which character's point of view is paragraph 7 written? Use examples from the passage to explain your answers.

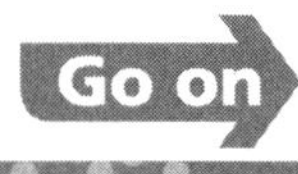

Copyright © by William H. Sadlier, Inc. All rights reserved.

Read the passage. Then answer the questions.

A Famous Pen Pal

1 Many students today have heard of Anne Frank. She and her family were Jewish. Because of this, they had to hide from the German Nazis during World War II. During that time, Anne kept a diary. It contains the typical dreams and problems of a young girl, but Anne also had unusual problems because of the war.

2 Before Anne and her family went into hiding in Amsterdam, she had a pen pal in the United States. Her pen pal's name was Juanita Wagner. Juanita was a student in Iowa. When Juanita's teacher gave her students a chance to write to other students in Europe, Juanita picked ten-year-old Anne Frank's name.

3 Juanita was also ten years old. She wrote to Anne about life on an Iowa farm, her sister, and her mother. A few weeks passed. Then Juanita received a letter back.

4 Anne Frank wrote about her family. She and her sister lived with their mother, father, and grandmother. She talked about her school, which let students decide how they spent their time on activities.

5 Anne included a postcard of Amsterdam in her letter. She told Juanita that she had a collection of about 800 postcards. Anne asked Juanita to include a photo in her next letter. She also asked Juanita if she knew another girl in Iowa who would like a pen pal. Anne had a friend in Amsterdam who wanted to exchange letters with an American pen pal.

6 Anne's letter to Juanita was dated April 29, 1940. Anne said she would continue to write to Juanita, but no other letters came. In May of 1940 Holland surrendered to Germany. Amsterdam became a very unsafe place for a Jewish family to live. A couple of months later, the Frank family went into hiding. They remained there for two years.

Copyright © by William H. Sadlier, Inc. All rights reserved.

7 Anne's father was the only family member to survive the war. He later found Anne's diary. It was published as a book titled *The Diary of a Young Girl*. The diary she wrote has been important in helping many people understand what life was like in Europe during World War II. The letters between Anne and Juanita are another example of the way that people can connect even when they are far apart.

33. In your opinion, what is the point of view of the author of "A Famous Pen Pal"? Give at least two details from the article to support your opinion.

Copyright © by William H. Sadlier, Inc. All rights reserved.

34. What details in "Two Worlds, Different but Alike" and "A Famous Pen Pal" help you understand the worlds of the pen pals?

35. Based on the two passages, "Two Worlds, Different but Alike" and "A Famous Pen Pal," is writing letters a good way to get to know someone new? Explain your opinion. Use specific details from each passage to support your opinion.

Copyright © by William H. Sadlier, Inc. All rights reserved.

Planning Page

You may use this space to plan your writing for question 36. Do NOT write your final answer to question 36 on this page. The notes on this page will NOT count as part of your answer to question 36.

Copyright © by William H. Sadlier, Inc. All rights reserved.

36. Reread "Two Worlds, Different but Alike" and "A Famous Pen Pal." Find examples in both passages of daily life. How are some parts of daily life in the present the same as they were in the past? How are some parts of daily life in the present different than they were in the past? Describe these similarities and differences. Use evidence from both passages to support your answer.

In your response, be sure to:

- ☐ Introduce the topic in your introduction.
- ☐ Use details from both passages to describe the similarities and differences in daily life in the past and present.
- ☐ Group related information together in paragraphs.
- ☐ Use transition words and phrases to connect ideas.
- ☐ End with a concluding statement or section.

Copyright © by William H. Sadlier, Inc. All rights reserved.

Stop

Copyright © by William H. Sadlier, Inc. All rights reserved.

Read the passage. Then answer the questions.

Family Ties

1 Jacob watched as Grandmother Martha looked through a stack of boxes from the closet. She was looking for old toys and clothes to donate to charity. Jacob's grandmother looked at a box all the way at the back of the closet. She smiled, but she also sighed sadly at the same time. She took out the box, opened it, and looked inside. Grandmother Martha pulled out an old watch and some papers that were yellow with age. "These are some of my grandfather's things," Grandmother Martha said. "Jacob, did I ever tell you about him?"

2 Grandmother Martha sat down on a chair with the box in her lap. She patted the chair next to her, and Jacob sat in it. "My grandfather, your great-great-grandfather," she said, "worked on the railroad as a Pullman porter. This was in the days before people could just hop on an airplane and travel wherever they liked. People really looked forward to being a passenger on a train. My grandfather Walter had a very important job."

3 Jacob's great-great-grandfather Walter worked on the railroad but not as a conductor or engineer. He worked as a porter. At the time, there were not many good, steady jobs available to African Americans. Pullman porters were known for being respectable men. Walter's job made people look up to him. He was able to travel all around the United States and see places that many of his friends and family would never get to visit. Traveling from place to place meant that he knew all the latest news, too. He got the latest newspapers from big cities all over.

4 Being a porter included many tasks. Walter took care of the passengers on the train. The train trips could last several days. The people stayed in rooms on the train. They were like hotel rooms, but these hotel rooms moved across the country. Walter made sure the passengers had everything they needed so that their trips were safe and comfortable.

Copyright © by William H. Sadlier, Inc. All rights reserved.

5 Being a porter was not easy. Walter worked many hours each day. He did not get many days off work to spend time with his family. Some passengers treated him disrespectfully, but Walter was a strong and proud man. He did not let the bad treatment distract him from doing a good job.

6 "He saved his money," said Grandmother Martha. "He started a family. Eventually he changed jobs and ran a business. He was the first man in the neighborhood to own his own business. He was able to make a nice home for his wife, his sons, and his daughters. One of his daughters was my mother." Grandmother Martha put the watch and papers back into the box.

7 "Times were very hard back then," she said, "and Grandfather Walter faced a lot of challenges. However, he did what he could so that his children, grandchildren, and great-grandchildren would have an easier life than he did."

8 "His great-great-grandchildren, too, like me!" said Jacob.

1. In paragraph 1, why does Grandmother Martha smile and sigh sadly at the same time?

A She is tired of working with Jacob even though she loves him very much.

B She is happy to find an object that reminds her of her grandfather, but she misses him, too.

C She had looked for this box for a long time, but then she forgot about it.

D The box reminds her of the stories her grandfather used to tell about respect and disrespect.

2. **Part A** Which best describes Walter?

A a conductor

B an engineer

C an adventurer

D a hard worker

Part B Which two statements support the answer to Part A?

I "Walter's job made people look up to him."

II "Walter worked many hours each day."

III "He did not get many days off work"

Copyright © by William H. Sadlier, Inc. All rights reserved.

IV "Walter was a strong and proud man"

V "'One of his daughters was my mother.'"

A Items I and II are correct.

B Items II and III are correct.

C Items III and IV are correct.

D Items IV and V are correct.

3. **Part A** In paragraph 1, the author uses the phrase ***yellow with age*** to show that

A the watch turned the papers yellow.

B the papers were always yellow.

C the papers are valuable, like gold.

D the papers are old and turned yellow over time.

Part B Which sentence from the story best helps you understand the meaning of ***yellow with age***?

A "Grandmother Martha looked through a stack of boxes from the closet."

B "Jacob's grandmother looked at a box all the way at the back of the closet."

C "'These are some of my grandfather's things,' Grandmother Martha said."

D "She was looking for old toys and clothes to donate to charity."

4. **Part A** Which sentences give the story's central messages?

I Travel by train is exciting.

II Kindness is important.

III Family is important.

IV Hard work leads to good results.

A Items I and III are correct.

B Items II and III are correct.

C Items II and IV are correct.

D Items III and IV are correct.

Part B Which detail supports a central message identified in Part A?

A "'However, he did what he could so that his children...would have an easier life than he did.'"

B "'People really looked forward to being a passenger on a train.'"

C "He got the latest newspapers from big cities all over."

D "At the time, there were not many good, steady jobs available to African Americans."

5. In paragraph 3, the author uses the phrase ***look up to him*** to show that Walter's job

A made people respect him.

B made him taller than others.

C made him stand above people.

D made people search for information about him.

Copyright © by William H. Sadlier, Inc. All rights reserved.

Read the passage. Then answer the questions.

Partners in Nature

1 In the wild, some animals hunt. Others are hunted. Did you know that some animals also help one another? Some protect one another. Others help one another get food. Some do both, like the sea anemone and the hermit crab.

Sea Anemone

2 A sea anemone is a small sea animal. It looks like a flower. Some sea anemones stick to rocks or other hard places. They do not move from place to place. They cannot move away if other animals try to eat them.

3 Sea anemones have colorful tentacles around their mouths. Tentacles are like arms. They are used to touch or grab things. A sea anemone's tentacles can have poison that stings or kills other animals. This is how the anemone protects itself.

Hermit Crab

4 A hermit crab lives in the sea, too. It has a soft body. It does not grow a hard shell. Instead, it lives in empty shells that other animals leave behind. It is sometimes hard to find a home. It is dangerous for a hermit crab to leave a shell. Other animals, like bigger crabs or octopuses, will eat hermit crabs if they get a chance. The hermit crab needs protection.

5 How does a sea anemone help a hermit crab? How does a hermit crab help a sea anemone? The hermit crab wears the sea anemone on its shell.

Safety

6 First, the hermit crab has to get a sea anemone. It is very hard to unstick an anemone, but the hermit crab knows exactly where to touch. The crab loosens the anemone from its rock. Then, once the anemone is free from the rock, it attaches itself to the crab's shell. Now the crab has a bodyguard. Sometimes, a hermit crab has two or even three sea anemones on its shell. The anemone's tentacles protect both animals from attacks.

Copyright © by William H. Sadlier, Inc. All rights reserved.

Food

7 In return, a hermit crab gets food for the sea anemone. The hermit crab finds food for itself. After the crab eats, the anemone eats the leftovers.

Mobility

8 Another way the hermit crab helps the sea anemone is by moving. On its own, an anemone can be trapped or stuck. On the shell of a hermit crab, it can move from place to place. This helps the anemone get more food.

9 By helping each other, hermit crabs and sea anemones also help themselves.

6. Part A Read paragraph 3 from the article.

> Sea anemones have colorful tentacles around their mouths. Tentacles are like arms. They are used to touch or grab things. A sea anemone's tentacles can have poison that stings or kills other animals. This is how the anemone protects itself.

What does ***tentacles*** mean?

A things like arms that touch or grab things

B colorful poison around the mouth

C a kind of sea anemone

D an animal that cannot move

Part B According to the article, what are tentacles used for?

A Tentacles help anemones move from place to place.

B Tentacles kill sea anemones.

C Tentacles protect an anemone from other animals.

D Tentacles add color around an anemone's mouth.

7. Which paragraph from the article best shows steps in order?

A paragraph 5

B paragraph 6

C paragraph 7

D paragraph 8

Copyright © by William H. Sadlier, Inc. All rights reserved.

8. **Part A** What is the purpose of the bold print subheadings?

A to emphasize the most important facts

B to highlight new vocabulary terms

C to tell what the text below will be about

D to add some new information to the article

Part B Which section of the article contains information on the eating habits of the sea anemone and the hermit crab?

A the section titled "Sea Anemone"

B the section titled "Hermit Crab"

C the section titled "Food"

D the section titled "Mobility"

9. **Part A** What does ***loosens*** mean in paragraph 6?

A unties

B disconnects

C punches

D turns

Part B Which two phrases from paragraph 6 support the meaning of ***loosens*** identified in Part A?

I "it attaches itself"

II "unstick an anemone"

III "is free from the rock"

IV "to the crab's shell"

A Items I and II are correct.

B Items I and III are correct.

C Items II and IV are correct.

D Items II and III are correct.

Copyright © by William H. Sadlier, Inc. All rights reserved.

Go on

Read the passage. Then answer the questions.

A Tricky Plan

1 Eldridge opened the tent flap for fresh air. His eyes took in the landscape of tawny lumps—as good as lumps of gold—dinosaur bones.

2 Eldridge's crew had been digging up dinosaur bones in Wyoming. They had telegraphed Connecticut about the newest batch of bones. The man named Marsh would buy them. Eldridge's team had to have the bones ready to load on the train at Medicine Bow. The bones would be shipped to Connecticut for Marsh.

3 The team would need to work fast. There were many buyers back East. Once they heard about the bones, their collectors would come to claim them.

4 So Eldridge poked his father, Joe, and whispered, "Sun's almost up! Let's get to work!" Then Eldridge went to wake the others.

5 It was not as if men could actually grab the bones and run off. Some bones were nearly as big as the railroad cars that would carry them. Others were tiny but all connected, like itsy-bitsy neck bones and wing bones. Far in the past, dirt had buried these bones. Then centuries of wind and rain uncovered them. Then some eagle eye had seen the lumpy Wyoming hills for what they really were, burial grounds and gold mines at the same time.

6 The morning passed with careful work. First, the men carved dirt away from the bones. Then, they wrapped the bones in plaster. After that, they packed them into crates. Wagons would take the crates to the depot at Medicine Bow.

7 At dusk, a wagonload of strangers lurched over the ridge to the east. The crew gathered to wait. "Who sent you?" Joe demanded. A man said, "Cope sent us to make sure these bones get to the right place."

8 Cope was Marsh's biggest rival. Joe's crew could keep Cope's men away from the bones they had already packed. Once the crates were on the train, though, Cope's men could pay the conductor to deliver the bones to Cope. Joe had faced Cope's agents before and knew what to do.

Go on

Copyright © by William H. Sadlier, Inc. All rights reserved.

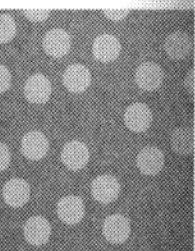

9 Eldridge was the answer. He snuck off in silence after dark. With him he had some cash the crew had saved from the last load of bones. Cope's men did not notice the boy's absence the next morning.

10 At the train depot at Medicine Bow, Eldridge paid the station agent to telegraph Cope. The unsigned message said, "Marsh lied. No bones in Wyoming." Eldridge knew Cope would believe it. He waited long enough in Medicine Bow to hire another boy. The boy delivered the reply to Cope's men: "Go to Nevada as soon as possible." The load of bones for Marsh would be safe.

10. What is a central message of "A Tricky Plan"?

A Dinosaur digs were hard.

B Dinosaur bones were of value.

C Dinosaur bone areas were secret.

D It is important to be prepared.

11. **Part A** Which of Cope's character traits solves Eldridge's problem?

A Cope's trust in telegraph messages

B Cope's desire for dinosaur bones

C Cope's detailed instructions to his men

D Cope's hatred of Marsh

Part B Which story detail shows the character trait identified in Part A?

A "Cope was Marsh's biggest rival."

B "'Let's get to work!'"

C "'Go to Nevada as soon as possible.'"

D "'Marsh lied. No bones in Wyoming.'"

12. What does ***eagle eye*** mean in paragraph 5?

A a bird seeking food

B a single bird eye

C a man looking for easy money

D a smart observer

Copyright © by William H. Sadlier, Inc. All rights reserved.

Read the passage. Then answer the questions.

Dinosaurs and Disrespect

1 Fighting in public does not make people popular. In the late 1800s, two fossil experts had a very public fight. To this day, they are more famous for their fight than for their dinosaur discoveries.

2 After the Civil War, workers laid track for a new railroad. It would link Nebraska and California. Crews began to hear about dinosaur bones in the hills of Colorado and Wyoming. Erosion had worn away old rocks and exposed the bones, as the drawing shows. Teams of men started collecting the bones and sending them east on the new railroad.

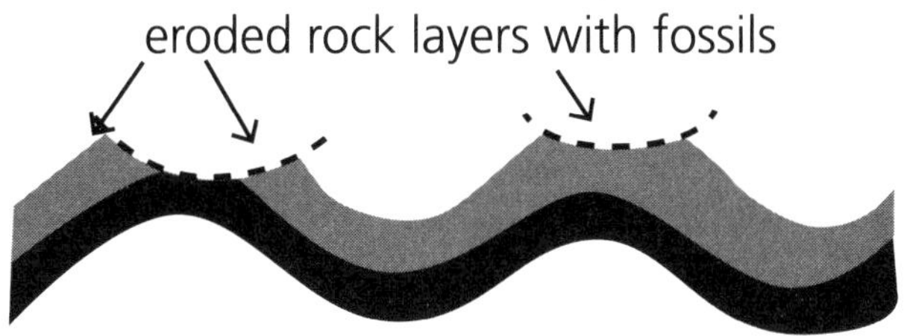

3 Othniel Marsh and Edward Cope grew up in the East. Both became experts at piecing together dinosaur bones. Both grew famous for naming dinosaurs no one had seen before. They were friends until 1870. Then Cope made a mistake.

4 Using bones from Kansas, Cope drew an ancient reptile called *Elasmosaurus*. By mistake, Cope drew the animal's head on its tail instead of on its neck. Marsh learned about the error and made fun of Cope. Cope tried to correct the mistake, but Marsh would not let it go.

5 Soon Cope and Marsh were trying to outdo each other. There was a "dinosaur rush" in the 1870s. The rivals hired collectors to find dinosaur bones in the West. The collectors, in turn, hired workers to get the bones and ship them east. Cope and Marsh also hired spies and double agents to keep each other from getting ahead.

6 Cope and Marsh raced to name their discoveries. They would not share information. As a result, many dinosaurs ended up with more than one name. It took years for other experts to sort the mess out.

Copyright © by William H. Sadlier, Inc. All rights reserved.

7 The men found other ways to fight. Sometimes after Cope's men were done taking bones from an area, they would blow it up. Any bones left would be impossible to get out. Meanwhile, Marsh took charge of a government department. Soon the government stopped hiring Cope to work on projects. Back and forth their rivalry went.

8 Finally, in 1890, Cope wrote a full-page newspaper account of everything Marsh did wrong. A week later, Marsh wrote his own full-page reply. Marsh tried to make Cope seem sloppy. After that, when people heard the names Cope and Marsh, they talked about their fight. Dinosaur work slipped into the background.

9 Cope died in 1897 and Marsh died in 1899. At that point, other experts could begin clearing up their real mistakes.

13. Which word and its definition most closely relate to the main idea of "Dinosaurs and Disrespect"?

A rivalry: competition

B famous: well known

C error: wrong information

D experts: people with special knowledge or skills

14. **Part A** Which describes the correct event sequence?

A Cope and Marsh were rivals until 1870. Then they became friends.

B Cope and Marsh were friends at first. Then they became rivals during the 1870s.

C Cope and Marsh did not meet until 1870. Then they became friends during the 1870s.

D Cope and Marsh were friends until 1870. Then they became rivals after disagreeing on the best way to find dinosaur bones.

Copyright © by William H. Sadlier, Inc. All rights reserved.

Part B Which detail supports the event sequence identified in Part A?

A "Fighting in public does not make people popular."

B "Erosion had worn away old rocks and exposed the bones"

C "Soon Cope and Marsh were trying to outdo each other."

D "other experts could begin clearing up their real mistakes"

15. Based on the drawing and the article text, where were dinosaur bones found?

A in the fields of Nebraska and California

B in the eroded rock layers of the East

C on the tops of eroded hills in Colorado and Wyoming.

D in the soil of California, Kansas, and Wyoming

16. Which detail from "A Tricky Plan" is supported by a fact in "Dinosaurs and Disrespect"?

A "The team would need to work fast."

B "First, the men carved dirt away from the bones."

C "Then, they wrapped the bones in plaster."

D "Then centuries of wind and rain uncovered them."

17. Which paragraph of "Dinosaurs and Disrespect" supports paragraphs 2 and 3 from "A Tricky Plan"?

A paragraph 2

B paragraph 3

C paragraph 5

D paragraph 6

18. Based on paragraph 5 of "Dinosaurs and Disrespect," which type of job do Eldridge and Joe in "A Tricky Plan" have?

A buyer

B worker

C spy

D double agent

Copyright © by William H. Sadlier, Inc. All rights reserved.

Read the passage. Then answer the questions.

Living History

The museum hall is grand and still.
The visitor can feel a thrill.
All around, displays and cases
Filled with fossil bones and traces—
Left behind as evidence
Of life before human presence.
Proof that creatures long ago
Walked and swam, fast and slow.

We see their tracks; we hold their bones.
Their bodies have been turned to stone
Or left impressions like a cast,
That serve as clues to the ancient past.

This is a leaf—or is it lace?
What creature could have left this trace?
Ancient seabed made of sand
Has turned to rocks and made a land
Dry and dusty, bright and hot.
From these fossils we learn a lot!

Copyright © by William H. Sadlier, Inc. All rights reserved.

Go on

19. How many stanzas make up this poem?

A two

B three

C eight

D eighteen

20. **Part A** How is the phrase ***have been turned to stone*** (line 10) used in the poem?

A It is used literally to describe how fossils form.

B It is used literally to describe how scientists find fossils.

C It is used nonliterally to describe what fossils look like.

D It is used nonliterally to describe scientists who work with fossils.

Part B What does ***have been turned to stone*** refer to in the poem?

A the museum hall

B the visitor

C displays and cases

D creatures long ago

21. How is the line ***This is a leaf—or is it lace?*** (line 13) used in the poem?

A It is used literally to describe a tool scientists use.

B It is used literally to describe part of a tree.

C It is used nonliterally to describe part of the desert.

D It is used nonliterally to describe the way a fossil looks.

Copyright © by William H. Sadlier, Inc. All rights reserved.

22. Based on the poem, draw a line from each item in the Central Message column to each item in the Key Details column that helps support that message. A central message may be revealed through multiple key details.

Central Message

1 There are different kinds of fossils.

2 We can learn about the past from fossils.

Key Details

a "Left behind as evidence"

b "Their bodies have been turned to stone"

c "Proof that creatures long ago"

d "Or left impressions like a cast"

e "That serve as clues to the ancient past"

23. Write numbers 1–3 on the lines to show the order of ideas presented in the stanzas of the poem.

_____ Animals' bodies are transformed into fossils over time.

_____ People acquire knowledge from looking at fossils.

_____ Ancient living things move around in their habitat.

Stop

Copyright © by William H. Sadlier, Inc. All rights reserved.

Read the passage. Then answer the questions.

My First Chinese New Year

1 Ling and I sit next to each other in homeroom. She just started at our school this past September, and we have become fast friends.

2 One morning in late January, Ling leaned across the aisle and poked me playfully in the arm.

3 "Hey, Emily," she whispered, "my mom asked me to invite you over for Chinese New Year. It's next Friday night. I hope you can come. It's so much fun!"

4 That night, I asked my parents if I could go, and they said yes. I was both excited and a little nervous. I had never been to a Chinese New Year celebration before.

5 On the night of the celebration, my mom dropped me off at Ling's house. After I got out of the car, Mom handed me two small bags. One bag was filled with oranges, the other with tangerines. Tucked inside the bag of tangerines was a red envelope with shiny gold Chinese characters. Inside the envelope was some "good luck" money. These were gifts for Ling's parents, the party's hosts.

6 Just as I rang the doorbell, Ling swung the door open wide and flashed me a huge grin.

7 "Em, you're here! Come on in!" Ling hollered above the hubbub coming from inside.

8 The house was filled with members of Ling's family. Ling introduced me to everyone. There was Grandpa Leung and Grandma Ziu. Both of them greeted me in Cantonese and beamed when Ling told them I was her new friend from school. Grandma Ziu's twinkling eyes and wide smile reminded me of Grandma Walters, my dad's mom.

9 I met Ling's mom and dad and presented them with the gifts my mom had given me. They thanked me and smiled warmly. Ling told me that oranges and tangerines are traditional symbols of happiness in China. She also said that giving "lucky money" in a red envelope, or *lai see*, is a custom during Chinese New Year.

Copyright © by William H. Sadlier, Inc. All rights reserved.

10 I also met Ling's older sister, Mei; her aunt and uncle; and her little cousin, Jian. Jian is about the same age as my younger brother, Henry. All of Ling's extended family lives together, which sounds like a lot of fun. I see my grandparents, aunts, uncles, and cousins only once or twice a year, when we visit Florida.

11 The party took place in the living and dining rooms. Everywhere I looked, I saw vases of colorful flowers. Red and gold paper decorations were hung on the walls. Ling explained that red symbolizes life and gold symbolizes good fortune.

12 Later in the evening, we sat down to a delicious meal. It reminded me of Thanksgiving dinner at our house, except there was no turkey, stuffing, or pumpkin pie. Instead, there were meat dumplings, chicken, a whole fish, long noodles, and sticky rice cakes. The sweet rice cakes were my favorite!

13 It was late by the time my dad picked me up. "Did you have a good time, Em?" he asked.

14 "I sure did," I murmured sleepily. "Happy Chinese New Year!"

24. According to the story, what do oranges and tangerines traditionally symbolize in China?

A good luck

B happiness

C courage

D loyalty

25. What does ***fast*** mean in paragraph 1?

A quick

B uncertain

C close

D cautious

26. Why was the narrator a little nervous about going to the Chinese New Year celebration?

A She did not know Ling very well.

B She had never been to a Chinese New Year celebration before.

C She did not enjoy the previous Chinese New Year celebration she attended.

D She knew her parents did not want her to attend the celebration.

Copyright © by William H. Sadlier, Inc. All rights reserved.

27. What does the word ***hubbub*** mean in paragraph 7?

A silence

B noise

C whispering

D neatness

28. Write numbers 1–5 on the lines to show the correct sequence of story events, from what happens first (1) to what happens last (5).

_____ Emily presents gifts to Ling's parents.

_____ The partygoers sit down to eat dinner.

_____ Emily meets Ling's sister, aunt, uncle, and cousin.

_____ Ling introduces Emily to her grandparents.

_____ Ling explains what two types of fruit symbolize.

Copyright © by William H. Sadlier, Inc. All rights reserved.

29. From whose point of view is the story told, an outside narrator or a story character? How is this point of view different from your own?

30. What do you think is one central message of the story? Support your opinion with at least two details from different parts of the story. Include the paragraph number for each detail.

Copyright © by William H. Sadlier, Inc. All rights reserved.

Planning Page

You may use this space to plan your writing for question 31. Do NOT write your final answer to question 31 on this page. The notes on this page will NOT count as part of your answer to question 31.

Copyright © by William H. Sadlier, Inc. All rights reserved.

31. Who are the two main characters in the story? How does the writer use details to convey each character's traits and feelings to the reader? Write at least three paragraphs to answer these questions. Reread the story and identify what each character says, thinks, feels, and does. Begin your essay by introducing the topic. Use story details to develop the topic, and group related information together. Use paragraph numbers to show where details are found in the story. Link your ideas with transition words and phrases, such as *also* and *for example*. End with a concluding statement or section that relates to the topic.

In your response, be sure to:

- ☐ Introduce the two main characters in your introduction.
- ☐ Use story details to describe each character's traits and feelings.
- ☐ Group related information together.
- ☐ Use transitions to link ideas.
- ☐ End with a concluding statement or section.

Copyright © by William H. Sadlier, Inc. All rights reserved.

Copyright © by William H. Sadlier, Inc. All rights reserved.

Read the passage. Then answer the questions.

Dex to the Rescue

1 Last summer, my grandma and grandpa and uncle and aunt and cousins moved into the house next door. They came from California. All of a sudden, my family had lots more people in it.

2 The grown-ups were happy. After supper, they sat in our backyard. Grandpa would tell stories in Hmong, and the grown-ups and my cousins would laugh. Grandma liked to sit with her feet in the wading pool and pet my dog, Dex.

3 My cousins came over almost every day. They really liked Dex. Unless I stopped them, they took Dex next door. Grandma and Grandpa also liked Dex. My aunt complained about the dog hair, but she liked Dex, too.

4 Grandma and Grandpa started grocery shopping for my aunt. My sister walked with them the first time to show them the way. They went to the store every morning. Then they started walking to the Asian Center after lunch. Grandpa asked me along once to meet their friends. I went, but it was boring.

5 School started. We kids got colds, one after another. My mother and my aunt took turns taking care of us. Around the middle of September, Grandpa caught the cold. He could not go outside, but Grandma wanted to do the shopping, so off she went. The problem was, she did not come back.

6 My aunt called my mom, my mom called my dad, and my dad and my uncle came home. When I got home from school, everyone was next door. I took Dex and went over. My uncle was on the phone with the Asian Center.

7 "She left at about ten...Could you ask if anyone saw her?" he said. There was silence. "She went by herself...She has gone many times... OK, OK. Thanks." He hung up. He turned to us and said, "She must have gotten lost. We'll have to look for her."

Copyright © by William H. Sadlier, Inc. All rights reserved.

8 Dad started organizing the search. Grandpa led Dex over to the chair Grandma likes to sit in. He said something in Hmong, and Dex's ears went up. Grandpa said it again and Dex went to the door. I opened it, and Dex raced out. "Hey!" I called. No one heard me. So I went after Dex, but the dog had already disappeared.

9 I walked for five or six blocks, calling Dex's name. After that I just kept walking in silence. I had no idea where to look, and I started to really worry about Dex. Then I heard the bark. It was to the left, in the park. I stopped and listened. The bark came again and I walked toward it. Then I found Dex and Grandma.

10 They were sitting next to each other. Grandma was petting Dex. When Dex barked, she would jump a little, and then she would pet Dex some more. She was sitting on the grass with her feet in the water of a little pond. I walked up, then sat down and petted Dex, too. Grandma looked over at me and smiled. "I'm glad you're here," she said in Hmong.

Copyright © by William H. Sadlier, Inc. All rights reserved.

32. In a paragraph, describe the narrator's point of view toward the grandparents. Use details from the story. At the end, say how your own point of view about the grandparents is the same or different.

Go on

Copyright © by William H. Sadlier, Inc. All rights reserved.

Read the passage. Then answer the questions.

Lifesaving Dogs

1 Dogs can save lives. Sometimes this happens by accident, but often dogs save people as a job. Two groups of dogs work as lifesavers: the searchers and the helpers.

Searchers

2 Searchers use their noses to find people who are lost or trapped. There are three kinds of search dogs: rubble searchers, area searchers, and trackers. Rubble searchers look for people in buildings that have fallen down. They are good climbers. They can also crawl into small spaces.

3 Area searchers hunt for human smells. They might search for hikers who are lost or hurt. Many times, these dogs do not find people, and that is good. It means that searchers do not have to look in that area any more.

4 Trackers look for just one person. They can follow the path a lost person took. These dogs sniff an object that belonged to the person and then follow that scent.

Helpers

5 Dogs that help people are either service dogs or companion dogs. A helper dog works for just one person. When it is on the job, it ignores everything but that person.

6 Service dogs guide people, help people get from place to place, and protect people from danger. Some service dogs use their eyes and ears. Others use their noses. For example, some dogs use their noses to keep a person from getting sick. One such dog can smell when its person's blood is starting to have too much sugar or not enough sugar. When this happens, the dog gets help right away.

Copyright © by William H. Sadlier, Inc. All rights reserved.

7 Dogs that guide and protect people are called full access service dogs. They stay with their people twenty-four hours a day, seven days a week. Often, they wear a vest or scarf that says what they do. The law says that these dogs are working animals, not pets. Places that do not allow pets, such as schools and restaurants, must let people have their service dogs.

8 Companion dogs help people in their homes. People who are sick or lonely feel better when these dogs are near. These dogs are not allowed in public places.

9 Companion dogs, service dogs, and searching dogs all save lives. They can ignore everything but the job they are there to do. Their work earns them praise and maybe, sometimes, a treat. Mostly, they are happy because they love to do their jobs.

33. Why do you think the author wrote "Lifesaving Dogs"? Which details help you decide why the author wrote the article? From your point of view, what would you add to the article to make it more interesting? Write a paragraph to answer the questions. Begin with your opinion on the author's reason for writing. Use details from the article to explain the reason. Then give your point of view on how you would add to the article, and explain your reason.

Copyright © by William H. Sadlier, Inc. All rights reserved.

34. What effect does Dex have on Grandma and Grandpa in "Dex to the Rescue"? Use examples from the story in your answer. Then tell which type of dog in "Lifesaving Dogs" is like Dex. Explain your choice.

35. In a paragraph, answer the following questions: What is the central message of "Dex to the Rescue"? What are two key details that convey this message? What is the main idea of "Lifesaving Dogs"? What are two key details that support this main idea?

Copyright © by William H. Sadlier, Inc. All rights reserved.

Planning Page

You may use this space to plan your writing for question 36. Do NOT write your final answer to question 36 on this page. The notes on this page will NOT count as part of your answer to question 36.

Copyright © by William H. Sadlier, Inc. All rights reserved.

36. Write three to five paragraphs to answer the following question: What kind of lifesaving dog would most help the characters in "Dex to the Rescue"? In your answer, use details from the story to explain the kind of help that the characters need, even though they already have Dex. Then refer to "Lifesaving Dogs" for ideas about the different kinds of dogs. Describe the type of dog that would help the most. Give the reason for your choice using details from the article.

In your response, be sure to:

- ☐ Introduce the topic in your introduction.
- ☐ Use story details to explain what kind of help the characters need.
- ☐ Use article details to describe what type of dog could help the characters.
- ☐ Group related information together.
- ☐ Use linking words and phrases to connect ideas.
- ☐ End with a concluding statement or section.

Copyright © by William H. Sadlier, Inc. All rights reserved.

Stop

Copyright © by William H. Sadlier, Inc. All rights reserved.

Read the passage. Then answer the questions.

Visiting the Past

1 "Old Jeremiah was a self-educated man. Do you know what that means?" Jeremy's Aunt Ida asked. She did not wait for an answer. "It means he taught himself. He didn't have a teacher or a school. But he fixed that for his kids and theirs."

2 Ida often told Jeremy stories about Old Jeremiah. Jeremy loved them. They were about the man he was named after. They all took place in Cahawba, the first capital of Alabama. It later became the county seat. After the Civil War, when Cahawba was a safe place for freed slaves, the first Jeremiah started a family.

3 "Cahawba was booming in 1859. Over three thousand people lived there," Ida said. "Most of them were African American. Then, the Civil War came. The South took the iron from the railroad. The army took the materials that made up the buildings. Then, the floods hit. In the end, there wasn't much left beyond a few houses and the old courthouse. But after the war, the African Americans who were now free made Cahawba their own. The population dropped to around 300, but the freedmen met there and fought for rights for their people."

4 Jeremy and his parents decided to visit Cahawba. He would finally get to see where the stories handed down by the family had taken place. He would see where mansions once sat. He would walk on the streets that Old Jeremiah, his great-great-great-grandfather, had walked on. He would see the courthouse where his family went to political meetings. He would see where his family went to school—a school that Old Jeremiah helped build.

5 Jeremy's mother warned him not to expect too much. Cahawba was, after all, in ruins. It was not even a ghost town. The town was gone. It had been flooded and abandoned. The state made it an archeological site. Jeremy did not worry. He knew how central Cahawba was to his history.

Copyright © by William H. Sadlier, Inc. All rights reserved.

6 The family got there in the morning. "Wow! Look at this!" Jeremy pointed to an enormous foundation. Only the stones of the building's base were left. Even so, Jeremy could imagine how grand the building looked nearly two hundred years ago.

7 Jeremy walked through the forest that used to be Alabama's capital. The stories of horses pulling carts came to life. He imagined all the freedmen meeting in the courthouse. He pictured the man he was named for leading the meeting. He could almost hear his relative's voice calling the men to action.

8 Jeremy felt good. He was a little disappointed that nothing was left but stones, though. Then, he turned the corner. There stood a building he recognized from the stories. This was the schoolhouse that Old Jeremiah and the other freedmen had built with their own hands.

9 Jeremy smiled, looking at the school. If his great-great-great-grandfather and others like him had not fought for education and equal rights, Jeremy would not be enjoying the life he had today.

10 "Thanks, Gramps," Jeremy whispered as he and his family left Cahawba.

1. The story's central message is about the power of family history. Which two details from the story best help support this message?

I "'Old Jeremiah was a self-educated man. Do you know what that means?' Jeremy's Aunt Ida asked."

II "Jeremy's mother warned him not to expect too much."

III "He knew how central Cahawba was to his history."

IV "If his great-great-great-grandfather and others like him had not fought for education and equal rights, Jeremy would not be enjoying the life he had today."

V "'Thanks, Gramps,' Jeremy whispered as he and his family left Cahawba."

A Items I and II are correct.

B Items I and V are correct.

C Items II and IV are correct.

D Items III and IV are correct.

Copyright © by William H. Sadlier, Inc. All rights reserved.

2. **Part A** How does Jeremy feel about Old Jeremiah?

A He is not interested in him.

B He has a negative opinion.

C He feels grateful.

D He does not know him.

Part B Which detail from the story helps you answer Part A?

A Jeremy is named after his great-great-great grandfather.

B Jeremy likes to hear Aunt Ida tell stories.

C Jeremy and his family visit the town of Cahawba.

D Jeremy says, "Thanks, Gramps" at the end.

3. **Part A** In paragraph 1, What does ***self-educated*** mean?

A educated by one's own efforts

B taught at home by the family

C educated on a job

D taught by a personal tutor

Part B Which sentences from paragraph 1 help you answer Part A?

I "'Do you know what that means?' Jeremy's Aunt Ida asked."

II "She didn't wait for an answer."

III "It means he taught himself."

IV "He didn't have a teacher or a school."

A Items I and II are correct.

B Items II and III are correct.

C Items III and IV are correct.

D Items I and IV are correct.

4. **Part A** Which is a central message of the story?

A Storytelling is only for fun.

B Storytelling brings history to life.

C Families tell good stories.

D Young people enjoy stories.

Part B Which aspect of the story helps build the central message?

A Aunt Ida tells stories often.

B Jeremy loves family stories.

C Jeremy's mother warns him not to expect too much from the visit to Cahawba.

D Jeremy can picture the past from family stories.

5. What does ***booming*** mean in paragraph 3?

A making a loud sound

B doing something with force

C getting bigger or more popular

D complaining under pressure

Copyright © by William H. Sadlier, Inc. All rights reserved.

Read the passage. Then answer the questions.

Chloride, Arizona
A Living Ghost Town

1 What does "ghost town" bring to mind? Old abandoned buildings? Tumbleweed drifting across empty streets? No people in sight?

2 Chloride does have some of these attractions. It is the oldest mining town in Arizona and it is home to the state's oldest operating post office. However, there are plenty of people. In fact, around 20,000 people visit Chloride each year.

A Visit to the Cerbats

3 Chloride is in the Cerbat Mountains of northwestern Arizona. It is fewer than four miles east of U.S. 93 on Route 125. The Grand Canyon, the Hoover Dam, and the city of Las Vegas are nearby.

Chloride's Beginnings

4 In the 1840s, prospectors discovered silver chloride in the area. A town was founded there around 1863. Many mines opened. A post office opened. The town became a stop on the stagecoach route, and finally the railway arrived. The town's fate was sealed. Chloride was a mining boomtown.

The Rise of Chloride

5 Chloride became the county seat in 1871. Chloride reached its heyday in the early 1900s. Over seventy mines were working. The population climbed above 2,000. Chloride was home to a two-room jail, a bank vault, a pool hall, a post office, and a railway station.

The People

6 Chloride's population started to dwindle with World War I. World War II turned Chloride into a ghost town. The price of minerals fell while mining costs skyrocketed. Miners were off fighting the war.

Copyright © by William H. Sadlier, Inc. All rights reserved.

As a result, many mines closed. Without the mines, the people had no reason to stay. The population dropped again. Only around 150 people were left.

7 Since then, the local population has stayed below 400. The citizens of Chloride are mostly retirees and artists.

Attractions

8 Take a peek at some of Chloride's original buildings. You can step into the two-room jail to see what outlaws in the Wild West experienced. You can mail a postcard from Arizona's oldest operating post office. You can visit abandoned mines, but entering them is not recommended. You can step back in time with the reenactments of gunfights every Saturday at high noon. Finally, check out the cemetery in Chloride. It is over 125 years old and holds a wealth of history.

9 If you are interested in more modern entertainment, try camping, stargazing, hiking, biking, or horseback riding. Walk about the town to enjoy the yard art of Chloride residents, or travel just out of town to see the murals of Roy Purcell. Be sure to take in all of Chloride's stunning views.

6. **Part A** Reread paragraph 1. What does ***abandoned*** most likely mean?

A invisible

B in need of attention

C unused or left behind

D grown over with weeds

Part B Which word from paragraph 1 is the best clue to the meaning of ***abandoned***?

A buildings

B tumbleweed

C empty

D sight

Copyright © by William H. Sadlier, Inc. All rights reserved.

7. Which terms explain how the ideas in paragraph 6 are connected?

I Compare and contrast

II Cause and effect

III Order of events

IV Order of importance

A Items I and II are correct.

B Items II and III are correct.

C Items II and IV are correct.

D Items III and IV are correct.

8. **Part A** Where in the passage would you look to find sights that attract travelers to Chloride?

A Paragraph 8

B Paragraph 6

C Paragraph 3

D Paragraph 2

Part B Which text feature is intended to be helpful in quickly locating information about attractions in Chloride?

A the title

B the section titles

C the paragraphs

D the dates

9. **Part A** In paragraph 4, what does the word ***prospectors*** mean?

A people who search for minerals to make money

B scientists who make discoveries about the earth

C people who travel west to find a new place to live

D government workers in the American West

Part B Which words from paragraph 4 give the strongest clues to the meaning of ***prospectors***?

A 1840s, area, town

B discovered, silver, mines, mining

C founded, opened, railway, fate

D post office, stagecoach, railway, boomtown

Copyright © by William H. Sadlier, Inc. All rights reserved.

Read the passage. Then answer the questions.

The Unexpected

1 At first, no one could explain what happened to people. The city had been like any other big city. People rushed to work, kids went to school, and tourists visited the park. Seasons changed. Close neighbors knew one another by sight and sometimes by name, but people mostly kept to themselves. Then, the storm—or storms—began.

2 First came the winds that knocked down power lines and blew roofs off of buildings. Next, the rain hit. It rained for days and nights, flooding sewers and rivers. Streets and yards were underwater. Water seeped into the houses. Finally, the freezing cold arrived and stayed for six months. It was so cold that no snow fell during those months. Some people whined that it was the end of the world. Others knew that they just needed to work together to survive the difficulties before them.

3 The winds forced everyone inside. When their roofs blew off, people had nowhere to go but down. The flooding of basement apartments left tenants nowhere to go but up, so people were forced into the middle of buildings. Without electricity for heat, neighbors crowded together for warmth. In fact, they became roommates instead of neighbors.

4 Some people fought at first. Who got the most food? Who got to sleep on a bed? Who had the most water? Who refused to share supplies? All these questions plagued the neighbors. Then the people realized that the best way to make it through was to get along.

5 At last, strangers came together like a well-oiled machine. Each person took on a job. An older woman and man were in charge of keeping one small living space clean and organized. Three young people were in charge of taking a makeshift sleigh into the streets to find food. Several men and women took turns tending the fire and cooking food for everyone, and then the children washed the dishes. Grandparents entertained children while adults worked.

6 As scared as everyone was, they kept doing their jobs. One little boy asked every night, "Mom, will it be warm tomorrow?"

Copyright © by William H. Sadlier, Inc. All rights reserved.

7 His mother replied, "We can only hope." However, she had little hope after months of cold.

8 Then, one morning, the used-to-be strangers began to stir early. Something seemed wrong or maybe just different. That is when the little boy squealed, "Icicles! The sun is melting the ice!" The sound of dripping water had awakened everyone in the apartment.

9 Soon the floodwaters began to recede, returning to the river and leaving destruction in their wake, but the used-to-be strangers knew they would be fine. They would clean up. They would rebuild. They would renew. They would survive. They knew how to cooperate.

10. Which is a central message of "The Unexpected"?

A Working together is key.

B People rarely make friends in big cities.

C Hope is the best way to fight fear.

D Getting along with neighbors is sometimes hard.

11. **Part A** Why do characters in the story decide to work together?

A It becomes clear that the cold will last a long time.

B They always wanted to help their neighbors.

C They want to keep an eye on everyone.

D They are tired of fighting.

Part B Which detail from the story supports the answer in Part A?

A "Close neighbors knew one another by sight"

B "Others knew that they just needed to work together to survive"

C "Some people fought at first. Who got the most food?"

D "but the used-to-be strangers knew they would be fine."

12. Read paragraph 5. What does the phrase ***like a well-oiled machine*** most likely mean?

A covered in oil

B like machines or robots

C with difficulty and friction

D with smoothly working parts

Copyright © by William H. Sadlier, Inc. All rights reserved.

Read the passage. Then answer the questions.

A Little Cooperation

1 People work on teams to win games, finish projects, and help other people. We join groups because they are fun. We can get more done. Helping others makes us feel good, but why do animals form groups?

2 Scientists have studied the ways that animals cooperate. They look at the result of animals working together to figure out why they do it. Often teamwork helps the species—but not the individuals—survive.

3 Honeybees are great at teamwork. Thousands of bees work together to build a hive and keep it running. Each bee in the hive has a job to do. The leader of the hive is the queen. She must have babies that will become queens. The other bees make sure the queen has babies and survives. The drones fertilize the queen's eggs so that she will have plenty of offspring. Then, the drones die. The worker bees gather pollen, build the hive, and feed the queen and her babies.

4 Why would a bee give up its life for the queen? Dying does not help that bee at all. If we look at the big picture, we see that a bee makes that sacrifice for the good of the whole group. Even after it is gone, bees live on.

5 Whales also benefit from teamwork. They move from one place to another in large groups. They do not interact much, but they do get together to fish. Some whales make a bubble net to round up fish. Each whale eats around 5,000 pounds of fish a day, so it needs all the help it can get! Why whales work together is obvious: They get more to eat. This is part of survival for each animal and for whales in general.

Whales blowing a bubble net

6 The reasons for teamwork among chimpanzees are much harder to

Copyright © by William H. Sadlier, Inc. All rights reserved.

figure out. For example, chimpanzees within a group often fight one another. They compete for power in the group, but they will work together to fight off chimps from other groups. They also groom one another. They share food. They help one another when there is no direct reward. Some of the teamwork is about keeping land, getting food, and staying safe. Other examples are about social roles. The way they work together shows who is in charge.

7 Perhaps animals work together for many different reasons. Cooperation can help get work done, bring more food, and be fun and feel good. More research needs to be done before we know for sure.

13. What is the main idea of "A Little Cooperation"?

A Animals like to work together.

B Animals probably have many reasons for working together.

C People are the only animals that enjoy working together.

D No species would survive this world without teamwork.

14. **Part A** What happens as a result of whales creating a bubble net?

A They have more fish to eat.

B They catch bigger fish.

C One whale gets more to eat, but not the others.

D Each whale is sure to get 5,000 pounds of fish each day.

Part B Which sentence from paragraph 5 supports the claim in the paragraph's first sentence?

A "They move from one place to another in large groups."

B "They don't interact much, but they do get together to fish."

C "Each whale eats around 5,000 pounds of fish a day, so it needs all the help it can get!"

D "Why they work together is obvious: They get more to eat."

Copyright © by William H. Sadlier, Inc. All rights reserved.

15. According to the illustration, how do whales use bubbles to make a net?

A They blow bubbles to completely surround a group of fish.

B As a school of fish swims, the whales blow bubbles to break it up.

C Several whales stay still and blow bubbles while another whale chases fish.

D One whale blows bubbles to draw in fish while other whales circle the fish.

16. How are the characters in "The Unexpected" like the animals in "A Little Cooperation"?

A One person is a clear leader. Others support the leader.

B Both groups fight over who has the most food and best sleeping space.

C They work together to get food and stay safe.

D They face a disaster and its results.

17. Imagine that the author of the article asked people in the story why they worked together. Which would most likely be their answer?

A to have more fun

B to help other people

C to feel better about themselves

D to get more done

18. Which claim do key details in both the story and the article support?

A Overcoming challenges often depends on teamwork.

B Disasters force people and animals to work together.

C Teamwork is not always the best solution to a problem.

D Without challenges, we would not need teamwork.

Copyright © by William H. Sadlier, Inc. All rights reserved.

Read the passage. Then answer the questions.

Our Friend Ocean

Ocean is a constant friend
And neighbor of our shores.
She comes to visit every morning
On dainty feet of white frothy lace.
Ocean tiptoes in with her treasures—
Sand, and sunshine, and shells, and fun.
She leaves them on the beach for all
As she quietly leaves for home.

But storms make Ocean angry.
Her steps are no longer light.
She stomps up the shore in a rage.
She doesn't stop politely there,
But barrels in through our yards and doors.
Her waters flood our streets and homes.
As she retreats, she takes her sand with her,
Leaving only destruction behind.

How can we stay close to Ocean?
Can we ever calm her rage?
We need to understand her
And respect her as we build.
Then we can have a friendship
That protects all involved.

Copyright © by William H. Sadlier, Inc. All rights reserved.

Go on

19. What is the main idea of the poem's first stanza?

A The ocean brings us treasures every day.

B The ocean is like a giving friend.

C The ocean can be friendly or angry.

D We need to treat the ocean well to keep it happy.

20. **Part A** In line 8, what does ***quietly leaves for home*** mean?

A Ocean waves pull back from the shore.

B The neighbor must tend to her own home at dinner time.

C The ocean considers sand, food, shells, and fun to be trash she no longer wants.

D Because the ocean has dainty feet, her departure is nearly soundless.

Part B Which words from the first stanza support the idea that the ocean is quiet?

A constant friend, neighbor

B morning, sunshine, fun

C dainty, lace, tiptoes

D treasures, sand, shells, beach

21. Which word best defines ***barrels*** as it is used in line 13?

A tiptoes

B loads

C containers

D rushes

Copyright © by William H. Sadlier, Inc. All rights reserved.

22. Based on the poem, draw a line from each item in the Examples column to an item in the Key Idea column to show which examples illustrate each key idea.

Key Idea	Examples
1 Ocean as constant friend	a Takes sand
2 Ocean angry in a storm	b Floods
	c Sunshine
	d Fun
	e Leaves treasure

23. Write numbers 1–3 on the lines to show the correct order of ideas presented in the three stanzas of the poem.

_____ Things will be all right if people can respect the ocean.

_____ When the ocean is calm, it can bring good things to people.

_____ When the ocean is not calm, it can do a lot of damage.

Copyright © by William H. Sadlier, Inc. All rights reserved.

Stop

Name____________________________

Read the passage. Then answer the questions.

The Lucky Ones

1 After school, Camila told her mom about what she had learned.

2 "The Ring of Fire wraps all the way around the Pacific Ocean," Camila exclaimed. "Did you know the ring got its name from all the active volcanoes there?" She did not wait for an answer. "Even better, Chile is part of the Ring of Fire. Can you believe Miss Rojas lived right next to an active volcano? Isn't that cool?" Miss Rojas owned the knitting shop below Camila's apartment.

3 "Not only did she live right next to a volcano, she was there when it erupted," Camila's mom said.

4 "I must ask her to tell me the story," Camila declared, and she did the next time she saw Miss Rojas.

5 "That story is about more than a volcano erupting," Miss Rojas said. "It is the story of the biggest earthquake of the twentieth century. It also happens to be the story of how I came to America. Let's get some lemonade and sit down."

6 "The week before the earthquake, the people living in Valdivia, Concepción, and Puerto Montt spent half their time running into the streets because they were afraid of buildings falling down. That's what you do when the earth begins shaking," Miss Rojas explained.

7 "On May 21, 1960, the earth shook violently. That tremor was a foreshock. Foreshocks come before the strongest quake. The next day there was another big foreshock. This sent everyone into the streets again, thank goodness. Just a half hour later, the biggest earthquake of the twentieth century hit our homes." Miss Rojas closed her eyes and shook her head.

8 "What happened next?" Camila was sitting on the edge of her seat.

9 "May you never see anything so awful, Camila. I watched buildings crumble and catch fire. People screamed and cried. My sisters and I stood in the street holding one another. We didn't know what to do.

Copyright © by William H. Sadlier, Inc. All rights reserved.

10 "Before we could figure things out, the tidal wave hit. It was as if the ocean were going to swallow the whole coast. It is a miracle we lived!"

11 Camila felt so sorry for Miss Rojas and said so.

12 "We were the lucky ones," Miss Rojas replied. "Many people didn't survive. Between the earthquakes, the tidal wave, and the mudslides that wiped out whole towns, millions of people were left homeless. Just two days later, Puyehue erupted. The blast sent ash flying and lava flowing. Lava covered the coast."

13 "What did you do?" Camila asked.

14 "We tried to help people who were seriously hurt," Miss Rojas explained. "It was really scary, but we were fortunate. My mother's cousin had moved to the United States two years before. Without a place to stay or a city to stay in, we got in touch with her and made our way to America."

15 "Wow!" exclaimed Camila. "I sure am glad you made it out safely," she said. "How did you get to America? What did you do when you got here?"

16 "That is a story for another day, my dear," Miss Rojas said and took a long sip of her lemonade.

24. According to "The Lucky Ones," what causes Camila to ask Miss Rojas to tell her story?

A She loves Miss Rojas's stories.

B She wants to learn about an event that happened in the Ring of Fire.

C She wants to know more about the biggest earthquake of the twentieth century.

D She is curious about why Miss Rojas came to America.

25. What does "spent half their time running into the streets" in paragraph 6 mean?

A People had to run out of their houses often.

B People almost never had to run outside.

C Going outside during an earthquake can be dangerous.

D People were upset about spending time outside.

Copyright © by William H. Sadlier, Inc. All rights reserved.

26. Which two phrases in paragraph 7 help you figure out when the earth shook?

A "living in Valdivia" and "running into the streets"

B "they were afraid" and "the earth begins shaking"

C "On May 21, 1960" and "The next day"

D "the biggest earthquake" and "hit our homes"

27. Read this sentence from paragraph 12. What is most likely the meaning of ***mudslides***?

> Between the earthquakes, the tidal wave, and the mudslides that wiped out whole towns, millions of people were left homeless.

A a natural disaster related to mud and flooding

B a large, destructive wave from the ocean

C a muddy slide for people to play on

D another kind of earthquake

28. Draw a line from each character to the line of dialogue he or she speaks. A character may have multiple lines of dialogue.

Character

1 Camila

2 Miss Rojas

3 Camila's mom

Dialogue

a "Not only did she live right next to a volcano, she was there when it erupted."

b "May you never see anything so awful, Camila."

c "Even better, Chile is part of the Ring of Fire."

d "Before we could figure things out, the tidal wave hit."

Copyright © by William H. Sadlier, Inc. All rights reserved.

29. Based on details in "The Lucky Ones," who tells the story of the earthquakes and the volcano erupting? How do you know? How is this point of view different from your own? Use at least two details from the story in your response.

30. In your opinion, what is the most important message of Miss Rojas's story? Include at least three key details from the story that work together to support this message.

Copyright © by William H. Sadlier, Inc. All rights reserved.

Planning Page

You may use this space to plan your writing for question 31. Do NOT write your final answer to question 31 on this page. The notes on this page will NOT count as part of your answer to question 31.

Copyright © by William H. Sadlier, Inc. All rights reserved.

31. Write an essay that describes Miss Rojas. Use the character's actions and words to figure out what kind of person she is. Refer to sentences and paragraphs in the story to explain your thinking. Then tell how Miss Rojas's actions contribute to the sequence of events.

In your response, be sure to:

- ☐ Introduce the topic.
- ☐ Develop the topic with details from the story.
- ☐ Group related information about Miss Rojas together.
- ☐ Connect ideas with linking words and phrases.
- ☐ Restate your main point in a conclusion.

Copyright © by William H. Sadlier, Inc. All rights reserved.

Copyright © by William H. Sadlier, Inc. All rights reserved.

Stop

Read the passage. Then answer the questions.

Wild Wind

1 Once upon a time, way back when, before buildings reached the sky, wind and sky ruled the Great Plains. The animals and people who lived there knew they were just visitors on the land. They knew they must follow the rules of wind and sky if they were to enjoy their stay.

2 Every spring as the wind warmed and the grass grew green, hope sprang anew in the visitors. The brutal cold of the wind would chill their bones no more. The darkness of sky would grow shorter.

3 On the other hand, fear also sprang anew in the visitors. With the warmth and light and growth came the threat of Wild Wind. From year to year, the visitors did not know if Wild Wind would visit. When she did come, she would twist around, taking trees and grass and homes with her. She sometimes took animals and people—the visitors—as well.

4 So each year the visitors prepared for Wild Wind's visit. They gathered their remaining supplies from the winter. Then they began digging and digging. Only under the earth were they safe from Wild Wind. It was a hard job. It was a long job. It was a boring job. Yet the visitors knew it had to be done.

5 One year, a young visitor suggested the visitors were wasting their time. He thought that time could be better spent planting or hunting or even resting. He had never met Wild Wind in his short years. He talked and talked until he convinced several others he was right. Wild Wind had not come for seven years. She must be gone forever.

6 These visitors did not prepare. They just hoped that Wild Wind would never visit again. They watched their neighbors save and dig and sweat, and they mocked them for their unnecessary work. They were wasting their time! Yet the neighbors knew it had to be done. Wild Wind would return.

7 Wild Wind returned so hard and quick that the visitors barely saw her coming. She came that spring not once, not twice, but thirty times in four days.

Go on

Copyright © by William H. Sadlier, Inc. All rights reserved.

8 Many of the unprepared were taken by Wild Wind. Others begged the neighbors they had mocked for help. The prepared visitors were kind. They shared their earthen caves and meager supplies. They survived.

9 After the chaos, the wise visitors called upon the young one who had abandoned preparations. They did not yell. They did not shame him. They reminded him that lives were taken because of his laziness. They declared that Wild Wind demands respect. They explained that she would come when she liked and that the visitors' only hope was to be prepared for her arrival.

10 The next spring, the young visitor was one of the first to start digging when the ground thawed and the air warmed. He learned from his mistake. He would prepare for himself and would help his neighbors when he finished.

Copyright © by William H. Sadlier, Inc. All rights reserved.

32. Describe how the young visitor feels about Wild Wind at first. Describe how the wise visitors feel about Wild Wind. With which point of view do you agree? Use details from the passage to support your opinion.

Copyright © by William H. Sadlier, Inc. All rights reserved.

Go on

Read the passage. Then answer the questions.

Nature's Fury

1 We call tornadoes Nature's Fury. Winds race over 300 miles per hour around a mile-wide swirling vortex of rain, hail, thunder, and lightning. Tornadoes have earned their nickname.

2 Tornadoes love to visit Tornado Alley. It is a strip of land that runs north to south through the Great Plains. The spring weather is often perfect for tornadoes. The air from Canada is dry and cold. The air from the Southwest is dry and warm. In Tornado Alley, the dry air from Canada and the Southwest meets the warm, wet air from the Gulf of Mexico. The three work together to form tornadoes.

3 You might think no one would want to live in Tornado Alley, but many big cities are there—for example, Oklahoma City and its surrounding areas, including Moore, Oklahoma. In 2013 these areas made the news because of the storms.

4 A large number of tornadoes—and some of the strongest ones—have hit Moore. Tornadoes are ranked on the Enhanced Fujita (EF) scale, from a score of EF0 (light damage) to EF5 (total destruction). Since 1999, two EF5 tornadoes have hit Moore. Some EF3 and greater tornadoes have hit the area, too.

5 The first EF5 tornado hit Moore in 1999. Thirty-six people were killed. Over $1 billion in damage was reported. Wind speeds reached 301 miles per hour. The second EF5 tornado came in May of 2013. Twenty-four lives were lost, and two schools were destroyed.

6 Those two events make Moore newsworthy, but there is more to the story. In May 2003, Oklahoma City suffered from a two-day tornado outbreak. Six tornadoes showed up, which is not a lot. However, each day had an EF3 or greater tornado. Luckily, no one died, but the damage was great.

7 Then, just seven years later, fifty-six tornadoes struck the state in one day. Four were rated EF3, and two were rated EF4. Unfortunately, Moore was in the path of one of the most destructive ones. Two people died as a result.

Copyright © by William H. Sadlier, Inc. All rights reserved.

8 Why do tornadoes cause so much destruction? Tornadoes are hard to predict. Tornadoes form out of supercell thunderstorms. These are easy to predict. However, not every thunderstorm forms a tornado. Therefore, scientists must figure out which storms will make tornadoes.

9 In the meantime, people should be prepared. Every family should have a safety plan in place. They should practice the plan before a tornado hits because there is not much time to move. In 2013, people near Moore only had a sixteen-minute warning. People living in Tornado Alley might even build a special storm shelter. Though these plans are not foolproof, they can help.

33. Read "Nature's Fury." What was the author's purpose for writing it? What is the author's point of view? Is it the same as or different from your point of view after reading the article? Use at least two details from the passage in your answer.

____

____

____

____

____

____

____

____

Copyright © by William H. Sadlier, Inc. All rights reserved.

34. Explain how Wild Wind could be another name for tornadoes. Use details and examples from "Wild Wind" and "Nature's Fury" in your answer.

35. What lesson does the young visitor learn in "Wild Wind"? Name a key detail from the folktale that supports the lesson. Name a detail from "Nature's Fury" that relates to the lesson. Explain how the details are connected.

Copyright © by William H. Sadlier, Inc. All rights reserved.

Planning Page

You may use this space to plan your writing for question 36. Do NOT write your final answer to question 36 on this page. The notes on this page will NOT count as part of your answer to question 36.

Copyright © by William H. Sadlier, Inc. All rights reserved.

36. Explain how "Wild Wind" and "Nature's Fury" describe scientific concepts related to weather. Which presents the concepts more effectively, the story or the article? Use key details from each passage to support your reason and opinion. Organize your essay logically and use linking words to show relationships between ideas. End your essay with a conclusion.

In your response, be sure to:

- ☐ Introduce your topic, the presentation of scientific concepts.
- ☐ State your opinion about the topic in your introduction.
- ☐ Include reason(s) to support your opinion.
- ☐ Support your reason(s) with details from both passages.
- ☐ Include a conclusion.

Copyright © by William H. Sadlier, Inc. All rights reserved.

Stop

Copyright © by William H. Sadlier, Inc. All rights reserved.

Read the passage. Then answer the questions.

A Bell for the Cat

1 Young Mouse stood pressed against the wall. His paws trembled. His heart beat wildly. He could hear the cat prowling quietly around the barn, hunting for her dinner. He glanced at Brother Mouse next to him. Brother Mouse was curled into a ball, staring out with wide eyes. His fur moved up and down with each breath.

2 "Where is the cat now? Is the cat gone?" whispered Brother Mouse after a few minutes.

3 "I do not think she has left yet," Young Mouse replied. They listened closely for the cat's soft, padded footsteps. They stayed huddled where they were, behind a bale of hay, waiting until they could no longer hear her. Finally, it was quiet. The brothers stopped shaking and then sighed with relief.

4 "I wish I had known the cat was in the barn. I would have made sure to stay away," Brother Mouse said. "We never know when it is safe in here!"

5 "I know one thing for sure," said Young Mouse. "We have to find a way to protect ourselves when we come to the barn to eat."

6 Young Mouse began to think. He wished he could make a plan to keep the other mice safe. Then the other mice would admire him. They would see him as a wise leader. How wonderful that would be! Suddenly, an idea came to him.

7 That night, Young Mouse gathered all the mice of the farm for a meeting. He stood up and announced that they should make a plan that would keep all of them safe from their deadliest enemy, the cat. Young Mouse asked for ideas.

8 There was a lot of talk and chatter, but nobody had an idea to suggest. Finally, Young Mouse spoke. "I know what we can do," he said importantly. "We can tie a bell around the cat's neck. It will ring whenever she moves, so we will know when she is on her way to the barn." Young Mouse continued to stand proudly, with his head held high.

Copyright © by William H. Sadlier, Inc. All rights reserved.

9 The chatter among the mice began again. A group in the front row applauded. All of the mice were excited about the plan to tie a bell around the cat's neck, except for one. Old Mouse, the oldest mouse on the farm, slowly stood up. He looked around the room. Gradually, the other mice stopped chattering. Finally, Old Mouse spoke. "Who among you is willing to tie a bell around the cat's neck? Please step forward."

10 All of the mice were silent. No one moved a paw or an ear or a whisker.

11 Old Mouse spoke once more. "Ah," he said. "It is easy to suggest impossible solutions, is it not?"

12 The meeting ended. No one tied a bell around the cat's neck, and all the mice, including Young Mouse, continued to fear her.

1. What lesson is revealed in paragraphs 9 and 10 of the story?

- **A** The best ideas help others as well as yourself.
- **B** Not every idea is accepted the first time you suggest it.
- **C** When coming up with ideas, it is better to work with friends than to work alone.
- **D** It is easy to come up with a plan, but not so easy to make it happen.

2. **Part A** What is one reason Young Mouse wants to solve the problem of the cat?

- **A** He wishes he and the other mice could take over the barn.
- **B** He wants all the other mice to look up to him.
- **C** He is supposed to protect his baby brother.
- **D** He is tired of becoming fearful every time he hears the cat.

Part B Which two paragraphs support your answer to Part A?

I paragraph 1
II paragraph 4
III paragraph 6
IV paragraph 8
V paragraph 11

- **A** Items I and V are correct.
- **B** Items II and III are correct.
- **C** Items IV and V are correct.
- **D** Items III and IV are correct.

Copyright © by William H. Sadlier, Inc. All rights reserved.

3. **Part A** Read this sentence from paragraph 1 of the story.

> He could hear the cat prowling quietly around the barn, hunting for her dinner.

Which is the best meaning of ***prowling*** in this sentence?

A sneaking

B stomping

C meowing

D chasing

Part B Which group of words from paragraph 1 best supports the answer to Part A?

A "pressed against the wall"

B "paws trembled"

C "quietly around the barn, hunting"

D "moved up and down with each breath"

4. **Part A** What is wrong with Young Mouse's idea for warning everyone that the cat is near?

A The cat can easily find a different place to hunt for food.

B Mice cannot tie a bell around a cat's neck.

C Young Mouse is too proud to see that the others will not do what he says.

D Old Mouse does not support the idea.

Part B Which sentence from the story shows that the answer to Part A is true?

A "No one tied a bell around the cat's neck."

B "Old Mouse, the oldest mouse on the farm, slowly stood up."

C "'We have to find a way to protect ourselves when we come to the barn to eat.'"

D "'I wish I had known the cat was in the barn.'"

5. Read paragraph 11. Which of the following are examples of "impossible solutions" like the one in the story?

I the mice learning where they can hide from the cat

II the mice asking their enemy, an owl, to chase the cat away

III the mice putting a hungry snake in the barn

IV the mice choosing a different leader

A Items II and III are correct.

B Only item IV is correct.

C Items I and IV are correct.

D Only item III is correct.

Copyright © by William H. Sadlier, Inc. All rights reserved.

Read the passage. Then answer the questions.

How to Build a House of Grass

1 In the late 1800s and early 1900s, many people went to live in the Great Plains of the West. If their land was away from rivers, there were almost no trees. There was just one thing they could use to build a house—the ground.

2 That is when people learned how to build houses from the **sod.** The grass on the plains grew tightly, with tangled roots that held in dirt. It was very hard to cut apart. This made sod good for building walls that would keep the weather out.

3 The first step in building a sod house was clearing an area for the floor. Having a plain dirt floor helped keep bugs, mice, and snakes from hiding in the home.

4 Next, settlers had to dig up the sod. They used a cutting plow that was made for this purpose. Once the sod was dug, they cut it into strips. Settlers cut only enough to use in a single day, because cut sod dried out quickly. If that happened, the dirt would **crumble** out and the sod would lose a lot of its **strength.**

5 The third step was to build the walls. Walls were usually two or three strips wide. This made the walls thick and strong. It also kept the house cool in the summer and warm in the winter. Settlers placed the sod strips with the roots pointing up. They laid strips lengthwise for a few layers and then put a layer on crosswise to lock everything together.

6 While building walls, the settler had to leave openings for doors and windows. Settlers used wooden boards to make frames for the openings. The walls went up around the frames. The settler left some space above the top of the frame. This was especially important above the window openings. Sod was heavy. Without some space to **settle** into, it could **crush** a glass window.

Copyright © by William H. Sadlier, Inc. All rights reserved.

7 After the window and door went in, it was time to add a roof. If they could, settlers used cedar poles to support the roof. Bugs do not like cedar wood. Settlers covered the poles with long grass, other plants, and maybe even more sod.

8 Finally, the owner could cover the inside walls with newspaper, cloth, or plaster to help keep out **pests.** This also helped hold in the dust that came off of the drying sod.

6. **Part A** Which is the best definition of ***sod***?

A tightly packed dirt

B ground beneath a person's feet

C grass and roots in dirt

D healthy green grass

Part B Which sentences contain clues to the meaning of ***sod***?

I "The grass on the plains grew tightly, with tangled roots that held in dirt."

II "This made sod good for building walls that would keep the weather out."

III "If that happened, the dirt would crumble out and the sod would lose a lot of its strength."

IV "Settlers placed the sod strips with the roots pointing up."

V "Sod was heavy."

A Items I, II, and V are correct.

B Items I, III, and IV are correct.

C Items I, III, and V are correct.

D Only Item I is correct.

Copyright © by William H. Sadlier, Inc. All rights reserved.

7. Which phrase describes the way the ideas in paragraph 1 are organized?

A order of steps

B compare and contrast

C cause and effect

D topic and examples

8. **Part A** Which bold vocabulary word from the passage describes what sod could do to a glass window?

A crumble

B strength

C settle

D crush

Part B Which word is a context clue that helps answer Part A?

A heavy

B openings

C frames

D strong

9. **Part A** Which of the following terms is a good substitute for "bugs, mice, and snakes" in paragraph 3?

A layers

B pests

C other plants

D dust

Part B What phrases from the passage help you understand the similarity between "bugs, mice, and snakes" and your answer to Part A?

A "placed the sod strips" and "crosswise to lock everything together"

B "cedar poles to support the roof" and "maybe even more sod"

C "from hiding in the home" and "to help keep out"

D "Having a plain dirt floor" and "that came off of the drying sod"

Copyright © by William H. Sadlier, Inc. All rights reserved.

Go on

Read the passage. Then answer the questions.

Nebraska

1 The sky was blue and the wind was gentle. The corn grew so close that Liza could hear leaves rustle when the wind changed direction. Liza sat on the ground to watch her father work on the new house.

2 "Come on," her mother said as she appeared with the washtub. "I need your help with the wash." The day was so nice that wet clothes would dry in the afternoon breeze. Even though her father was cutting strips of sod, there was not much dust in the air.

3 "It has been almost impossible to keep things clean in the dugout," her father said. "With a sod house, much less dirt will get inside. In a few more years, we will have enough money to buy wood for a house and a barn."

4 Liza's mother sighed. "Free land sounded nice at first. Living here is not free, though. At least we could bring some seeds with us from Ohio. The people on the new farm have to buy their seeds this year. They asked if they could share our plow horse, too."

5 "We are all farmers," Liza's father replied. "We can help our neighbors get started. Last year we had a good crop. If the weather holds, we will have another good crop this year." He looked up at his wife and smiled. "Nebraska will be better than Ohio."

6 Back East, Liza's family worked land that someone else owned. When the government offered land in Nebraska for free, her mother and father decided to move. Liza missed the town and the trees in Ohio, but more than that, she missed her friends. "Do the new people have children?" she asked.

7 "I think they might," her mother said. "After we hang the wash, you can walk over to introduce yourself and find out." Liza helped her mother. Then she hugged her parents and set off for the next farm. On her way there, she stopped to look at some yellow flowers that reminded her of Ohio.

Copyright © by William H. Sadlier, Inc. All rights reserved.

8 "Those are coneflowers," a voice called. Liza spun around. A boy her age was walking toward her. "My name is Peter," he said. "My family is homesteading over there." He pointed south. "Who are you?"

9 Liza turned back toward the flowers. "My name is Liza. My family came last year. We lived in Ohio before. Where are you from?"

10 "New York City. My family had a flower shop. My parents decided to come here, learn to farm, and then own the land in five years. I think it is going to be hard work." Peter stood next to her and looked at the flowers.

11 "We have three years to go after this one," Liza said. "It is hard work, but my father says we will help you. You can teach me about flowers. I will show you how to help with the wash."

12 "I hope that is a joke!" said Peter with a smile.

10. Which is a central message of "Nebraska"?

A It is worthwhile to be polite to everyone you meet.

B Spending time with friends makes family life nicer.

C When you have the chance to get something for free, take it.

D A positive attitude can help build friendships.

11. **Part A** Which two words best describe the mother's feelings?

I forgiving

II angry

III curious

IV confused

V cooperative

A Items I and IV are correct.

B Items II and III are correct.

C Items III and V are correct.

D Items IV and V are correct.

Part B Which paragraph of "Nebraska" shows the mother's feelings from Part A?

A paragraph 7

B paragraph 6

C paragraph 3

D paragraph 2

12. What is the meaning of ***holds*** in paragraph 5?

A grabs on tightly

B stays the same

C contains an amount

D keeps safe

Copyright © by William H. Sadlier, Inc. All rights reserved.

Read the passage. Then answer the questions.

Homesteading on the Prairie

1 Between 1862 and 1900, over one million people moved to the Nebraska Territory. Some of them were farmers from the eastern United States. Others were former slaves and immigrants from Europe. Some were families, and some were single men and women. They all had one thing in common: they wanted to own land.

2 The United States had become bigger, and much of its land was not settled. The government wanted people to move there. Not many people could afford to buy land, so Congress passed the Homestead Act in 1862. The act said that anyone who moved to Nebraska would get 160 acres of free land. There were rules, however. They are listed in the table.

Homesteading Rules	Homesteading Challenges
To Own Your 160-acre Homestead, You Must • Move there within 6 months • Live there for 5 years • Never leave for longer than 6 months • Have no other legal residence • Build a dwelling: At least 10 feet by 12 feet with at least one glass window • Raise crops	• Grasshoppers • Drought • Blizzards • Hailstorms • Prairie Fires • High Winds

Copyright © by William H. Sadlier, Inc. All rights reserved.

3 This offer was popular. The people who did well on the new land were mostly those who already knew how to farm. Farming required seeds, water, and animals. Unless a person came from another farm, he or she had to pay for seeds. Early settlers claimed the land closest to the rivers, and for them getting water was fairly simple. Away from rivers, people had to dig wells for water. Sometimes the wells were so deep that settlers had to build windmills to pump water up. Animals cost money. Even if a farmer already had animals, he or she had to build fences to keep them from wandering away.

4 Farming the prairie was hard. Look at the table to see some of the challenges farmers faced. When farms failed, people left. In one four-year period, half of the people who lived on the Nebraska prairies moved away. Only one-third of the homesteaders from the 1860s to the 1930s lasted the five years required to claim the free land.

13. What is the main idea of "Homesteading on the Prairie"?

A In 1862, Congress passed the Homestead Act to encourage people to settle in the Nebraska Territory.

B Former slaves and European immigrants were two groups that moved to Nebraska with the goal of eventually owning land.

C Many people moved to Nebraska to get free land, but farming was so difficult that most left before gaining ownership of the land.

D Homesteaders in Nebraska were required to build a dwelling that was a minimum of ten feet by twelve feet, with at least one glass window.

14. **Part A** According to "Homesteading on the Prairie," what was one effect of the Homestead Act?

A The government wanted people to settle the Nebraska Territory.

B People purchased land near rivers in the states west of the Mississippi River.

C Only families, rather than single people, settled the lands of the West.

D People moved to Nebraska from other places.

Copyright © by William H. Sadlier, Inc. All rights reserved.

Part B Which factual information supports the answer to Part A?

A "Between 1862 and 1900" and "Congress passed the Homestead Act in 1862"

B "people who did well on the new land were mostly those who already knew how to farm"

C "Away from rivers, people had to dig wells for water."

D "only one-third of homesteaders had lasted the five years required to claim the free land"

15. Look at the table. Which of the following items did NOT cause people to leave their homesteads before five years were up?

I grasshoppers

II failure to grow crops

III having no other legal residence

IV bad weather

V building a ten-foot by twelve-foot dwelling

A Items II and V are correct.

B Items I and IV are correct.

C Items III and V are correct.

D Items I, II, IV, and V are correct.

16. Which is an important point in both "Nebraska" and "Homesteading on the Prairie"?

A similarities between eastern states and the Nebraska Territory

B Nebraska as a land of opportunity

C the hardships of farming far from water sources

D the loneliness of life away from families and friends

17. Which key detail about getting free land appears in both "Nebraska" and "Homesteading on the Prairie"?

A needing to build a wooden house

B planning ahead for the effects of bad weather

C having previous experience working on a farm

D having to stay on the land for five years

18. Based on information in "Homesteading on the Prairie," which is the best way Liza's family could help Peter's family in "Nebraska"?

A sharing a well with Peter's family

B giving Peter's family corn seeds

C teaching Peter's family how to farm

D helping Peter's family build a house

Copyright © by William H. Sadlier, Inc. All rights reserved.

Read the passage. Then answer the questions.

Homesteading Limericks

1

From Bohemia, cousin Jake crossed the sea
To farm land in Nebraska for free.
He fought bug, snake, and mouse
To construct the sod house
On his acres one hundred sixty.

2

A lady grew corn on her homestead
But no buyers would buy it, so she said
"I'll use leaves from my crop
For my sod house's top
And I'll bake all the grain into cornbread."

3

The grasshoppers came in a cloud.
With their clacking horrifically loud,
They destroyed the crop yields
At their feast in the fields
That the farmers had carefully plowed.

Copyright © by William H. Sadlier, Inc. All rights reserved.

19. These three five-line stanzas are limericks, a kind of poem that follows rhyming rules. Which statement below describes the rhyming rules in a limerick?

A Lines 1, 2, and 5 rhyme, and lines 3 and 4 are a different rhyme.

B Lines 1, 3, and 5 rhyme, and lines 2 and 4 are a different rhyme.

C All the lines rhyme with one another.

D Lines 1, 2 and 3 rhyme, and lines 4 and 5 are a different rhyme.

20. **Part A** Which is the best meaning of ***horrifically*** in line 2 of the third limerick?

A musically

B frighteningly

C pleasantly

D unfailingly

Part B Which of these words from the third limerick supports the answer to Part A?

A clacking

B carefully

C plowed

D destroyed

21. What does the word ***top*** mean in line 4 of the second limerick?

A toy

B cover

C roof

D shirt

Copyright © by William H. Sadlier, Inc. All rights reserved.

Go on

22. Draw a line from each item in the Limerick column to the items in the Key Ideas column that apply to that poem. Each key idea may apply to one or both limericks.

Limerick	Key Ideas
1 first limerick	**a** making an effort
2 second limerick	**b** thinking creatively
	c leaving home
	d overcoming difficulty
	e changing plans

23. Write numbers 1–5 on the lines to show the correct order of the lines in a new limerick.

_____ Was too clever for that,

_____ They would outfit the cat with a bell.

_____ The young mouse had a plan that was swell:

_____ So the mice had to learn how to yell.

_____ However, the cat

Stop

Copyright © by William H. Sadlier, Inc. All rights reserved.

Name ____

Read the passage. Then answer the questions.

Flowers

1 It was June, the last day of school, and Maya was telling her teacher she was heartsick because they had to move away.

2 They were going because Maya's father got sick every spring when the trees leafed out. Some days he could hardly breathe. They were moving to Tucson, thousands of miles away. Tucson had cactus and not so many trees.

3 Maya did not tell her teacher why she was really heartsick about the move. She had to leave her garden behind. She loved her roses and lilies nearly as much as she loved her family. Those flowers would not grow in Tucson. The city was in a desert and it was very, very dry.

4 They had to go, though, so they did. They took an overnight train to Chicago. Then they got on the Texas Eagle. They passed through St. Louis and Little Rock the first night, Dallas and San Antonio the next. As the train took them farther and farther from New York, Maya got sadder and sadder. By seven o'clock the third night, they were in Tucson.

5 Sandy, a real estate agent, met them at the station. Sandy was excited to welcome them to their new hometown. Maya's family was all smiles, but Maya was trying not to cry. By the time they got to their house, Sandy had to ask: "What is wrong, Maya? This is the start of a new life! Your family is going to love it here."

6 Maya's mouth quivered. "I miss my flowers," she said. "I am so sorry! I will get used to it, I know, some day."

7 Sandy stared for a moment. Then she said, "Back in the van!" Maya felt a little nervous. She wondered if Sandy was angry or upset. However, the family followed instructions. Sandy drove the van to a place called Saguaro National Park. They parked in a lot and then walked out into the desert. The edge of the land was just starting to turn orange with the sunset. Sandy led them to group of rocks and told them to sit.

Copyright © by William H. Sadlier, Inc. All rights reserved.

8 As the sun glowed and sank, more colors appeared. It wasn't just the sun on the rocks. It was flowers, flowers, and more flowers. The cactus had flowers. The towering saguaro had white-pink flowers at the tips of its arms. Sandy said, "Look at the pink flowers on the tall ones over there—those are organ pipe cactus. Look at the white flowers there. They look like water lilies, but they are on a cactus called senita. Maya," she continued quietly, "you will have flowers here. You just have to know where to look for them." As the night began to fill the desert, Maya thought to herself, "I am going to be happy here after all."

24. Which paragraphs of the story explain why Maya is sad?

A paragraphs 1 and 2

B paragraphs 3 and 6

C paragraphs 1, 4, and 5

D paragraphs 2, 7, and 8

25. Read paragraphs 1 and 3 of "Flowers." Which meaning of ***heartsick*** fits the way the word is used in the story?

A deeply sad

B unable to breathe

C very weak

D without hope

26. Where is Maya's family living when the story begins?

A in Chicago

B in a city

C in the country

D in New York

27. Which sentence from the story is an example of a figure of speech?

A "Some days he could hardly breathe."

B "She loved her roses and lilies nearly as much as she loved her family."

C "Sandy, a real estate agent, met them at the station."

D "The family was all smiles."

Copyright © by William H. Sadlier, Inc. All rights reserved.

28. Draw a line from each character on the left to an item on the right. For each character, find the one description that best matches the way he or she develops over time.

Character	How Character Develops
1 Maya's father	**a** teaches people about desert plants
2 Sandy	**b** guesses why Maya is sad
3 Maya	**c** finds something new to enjoy
	d changes from being sick to being happy

29. In the first three paragraphs of "Flowers," what does the reader know about Maya that the other characters do not know? Use a quotation from the story to explain.

____

____

____

____

____

____

____

____

Copyright © by William H. Sadlier, Inc. All rights reserved.

30. In what paragraph does the story describe the flowers in Maya's garden? In what paragraph does the story describe the flowers in Tucson? What is the main difference between the kinds of flowers? What lesson does this difference teach about how people can be happy? Use a detail from the story to support your answer.

Copyright © by William H. Sadlier, Inc. All rights reserved.

Planning Page

You may use this space to plan your writing for question 31. Do NOT write your final answer to question 31 on this page. The notes on this page will NOT count as part of your answer to question 31.

Copyright © by William H. Sadlier, Inc. All rights reserved.

31. In two or three paragraphs, tell whether or not you think Sandy treats the family correctly when they get to Tucson. Think about how Sandy behaves, what she says, and how the other characters react to her. Start your answer by introducing the topic and giving your opinion. Then describe Sandy. Use adjectives to tell what she is like and give examples from the story to illustrate your description. End your answer by giving your opinion again. Use a linking word to connect your opinion to the rest of what you have written.

In your response, be sure to:

- ☐ Introduce your topic—the character of Sandy in "Flowers."
- ☐ Give your opinion about the character's behavior.
- ☐ Include details about Sandy and how her actions affect the story.
- ☐ Give reasons for your opinion based on details in the story.
- ☐ Include an ending that connects your reasons and your opinion.

Copyright © by William H. Sadlier, Inc. All rights reserved.

Copyright © by William H. Sadlier, Inc. All rights reserved.

Stop

Read the passage. Then answer the questions.

Autumn Colors

Even with my crayons
And all colors of paint
I cannot re-create the
Shades of autumn's forest.

The oak that I climb on
In spring and in summer
Turns into a blazing orange sea
Of butterfly wings.

The towering birch tree
With its bark like paper
Stands white, gray, and peeling,
Its leaves the color of sun.

The massive red maple
Waves its huge branches
To reveal scarlet curtains
Of bright, fiery splendor.

Copyright © by William H. Sadlier, Inc. All rights reserved.

The small, wiry dogwood
Has shed its white flowers
And replaces them slowly
With royal purple gemstones.

But not all trees are changing.
Green branches of cedar
Will whisper like emerald feathers
Through winter's cold days.

Copyright © by William H. Sadlier, Inc. All rights reserved.

32. What does the author of the poem think about autumn colors? Use details from lines 1–4 to support your answer. Do you agree with the author's point of view? State at least one reason to support your opinion.

Copyright © by William H. Sadlier, Inc. All rights reserved.

Read the passage. Then answer the questions.

Leaf Science

1 The green leaves that many trees have in the spring and summer turn different colors in autumn. They turn red, orange, and yellow. What causes leaves to change color at this time of year?

2 The color of leaves comes from pigments. A *pigment* is anything that gives color to something else. Two leaf pigments are *chlorophyll* and *carotene*. They give a plant color. They also help the plant get food.

3 A plant's main source of food is sugar. Plants make their own sugar from sunlight. Chlorophyll and carotene help the plants use sunlight to make sugar. Chlorophyll is green. It is made when the weather is warm. Carotene is yellow or orange. It is made in warm and cold weather. When it is warm, leaves have both pigments, but you see only the green from chlorophyll. That is why the leaves are green in summer.

4 As the weather cools down, the tree stops making chlorophyll. Then you can see carotene. That's why leaves begin to change to yellow and orange in the fall.

5 What about red leaves? A few kinds of trees have leaves that turn red. This is because of another pigment, *anthocyanin*. Sometimes fall days are warm, but the nights are cold. Leaves make sugar during the day. At night, the cold temperature makes it hard for the leaves to send sugar to the rest of the tree. That is when some trees start to make anthocyanin. It protects the leaves from the cold. It allows them to keep sending sugar to the other parts of the tree. It also gives the leaves a crisp red color. It can even make leaves purple!

6 A fourth pigment, called *tannin*, gives leaves a brown color. Tannin is like carotene because it is always there in the leaf, but you can see only green from chlorophyll. Sometimes as chlorophyll goes away, leaves turn brown or brownish-yellow because of tannin.

Copyright © by William H. Sadlier, Inc. All rights reserved.

7 Most trees shed their leaves when it gets very cold. Any leaves that are still on the tree turn brown and fall off. Why does this happen? The leaves are no longer able to send sugar to other parts of the tree. The tree trunk, branches, and roots hold on to the sugar they have left. The leaves and the branches come apart. The tree lets go of the leaves. These leaves break down until they become part of the soil. As soil, they can still help to feed the tree. In spring, the tree grows an entire new set of green leaves.

33. The author of "Leaf Science" has put some words in *italics*, or slanted printing. Why do you think the author did this? If you were revising the article to share with your class, would you put the same words in italics? Write one paragraph to support your opinion.

Copyright © by William H. Sadlier, Inc. All rights reserved.

34. The final stanza of the poem refers to cedar branches. How does this stanza connect to "Leaf Science"? What question would you ask the article's author to clarify the stanza about cedar?

____

____

____

____

____

____

____

____

35. What is the central message of "Autumn Colors"? Give at least two key details that help you find the central message. What is the main idea of "Leaf Science"? Give at least two key details that help you decide on the main idea. Finally, in one sentence, say how the article's main idea is connected to the poem's central message.

____

____

____

____

____

____

____

____

____

Copyright © by William H. Sadlier, Inc. All rights reserved.

Planning Page

You may use this space to plan your writing for question 36. Do NOT write your final answer to question 36 on this page. The notes on this page will NOT count as part of your answer to question 36.

Copyright © by William H. Sadlier, Inc. All rights reserved.

36. How do "Autumn Colors" and "Leaf Science" explain the change of seasons? What steps happen when seasons change, and how does one step cause another step? Write three paragraphs to answer these questions. Begin by introducing the topic. Then organize your ideas to show how the passages describe the changing seasons. End your response with a conclusion about how the two passages help you understand the change of seasons.

In your response, be sure to:

- ☐ Include an introductory sentence with your topic.
- ☐ Provide examples of how each passage describes different seasons.
- ☐ Provide examples of how one or both passages explain the change of season.
- ☐ Include a conclusion about how the passages add to your understanding.

Copyright © by William H. Sadlier, Inc. All rights reserved.

Stop

Copyright © by William H. Sadlier, Inc. All rights reserved.

Name ______________________

Benchmark 1

1. Ⓐ Ⓑ Ⓒ Ⓓ
2A. Ⓐ Ⓑ Ⓒ Ⓓ
2B. Ⓐ Ⓑ Ⓒ Ⓓ
3A. Ⓐ Ⓑ Ⓒ Ⓓ
3B. Ⓐ Ⓑ Ⓒ Ⓓ
4A. Ⓐ Ⓑ Ⓒ Ⓓ
4B. Ⓐ Ⓑ Ⓒ Ⓓ
5. Ⓐ Ⓑ Ⓒ Ⓓ
6A. Ⓐ Ⓑ Ⓒ Ⓓ
6B. Ⓐ Ⓑ Ⓒ Ⓓ
7. Ⓐ Ⓑ Ⓒ Ⓓ
8A. Ⓐ Ⓑ Ⓒ Ⓓ
8B. Ⓐ Ⓑ Ⓒ Ⓓ
9A. Ⓐ Ⓑ Ⓒ Ⓓ
9B. Ⓐ Ⓑ Ⓒ Ⓓ
10. Ⓐ Ⓑ Ⓒ Ⓓ
11A. Ⓐ Ⓑ Ⓒ Ⓓ
11B. Ⓐ Ⓑ Ⓒ Ⓓ
12. Ⓐ Ⓑ Ⓒ Ⓓ
13. Ⓐ Ⓑ Ⓒ Ⓓ
14A. Ⓐ Ⓑ Ⓒ Ⓓ
14B. Ⓐ Ⓑ Ⓒ Ⓓ
15. Ⓐ Ⓑ Ⓒ Ⓓ
16. Ⓐ Ⓑ Ⓒ Ⓓ
17. Ⓐ Ⓑ Ⓒ Ⓓ
18. Ⓐ Ⓑ Ⓒ Ⓓ
19. Ⓐ Ⓑ Ⓒ Ⓓ
20A. Ⓐ Ⓑ Ⓒ Ⓓ
20B. Ⓐ Ⓑ Ⓒ Ⓓ
21. Ⓐ Ⓑ Ⓒ Ⓓ
22. //////////////////////
23. //////////////////////
24. Ⓐ Ⓑ Ⓒ Ⓓ
25. Ⓐ Ⓑ Ⓒ Ⓓ
26. Ⓐ Ⓑ Ⓒ Ⓓ
27. Ⓐ Ⓑ Ⓒ Ⓓ
28. //////////////////////

Benchmark 2

1. Ⓐ Ⓑ Ⓒ Ⓓ
2A. Ⓐ Ⓑ Ⓒ Ⓓ
2B. Ⓐ Ⓑ Ⓒ Ⓓ
3A. Ⓐ Ⓑ Ⓒ Ⓓ
3B. Ⓐ Ⓑ Ⓒ Ⓓ
4A. Ⓐ Ⓑ Ⓒ Ⓓ
4B. Ⓐ Ⓑ Ⓒ Ⓓ
5. Ⓐ Ⓑ Ⓒ Ⓓ
6A. Ⓐ Ⓑ Ⓒ Ⓓ
6B. Ⓐ Ⓑ Ⓒ Ⓓ
7. Ⓐ Ⓑ Ⓒ Ⓓ
8A. Ⓐ Ⓑ Ⓒ Ⓓ
8B. Ⓐ Ⓑ Ⓒ Ⓓ
9A. Ⓐ Ⓑ Ⓒ Ⓓ
9B. Ⓐ Ⓑ Ⓒ Ⓓ
10. Ⓐ Ⓑ Ⓒ Ⓓ
11A. Ⓐ Ⓑ Ⓒ Ⓓ
11B. Ⓐ Ⓑ Ⓒ Ⓓ
12. Ⓐ Ⓑ Ⓒ Ⓓ
13. Ⓐ Ⓑ Ⓒ Ⓓ
14A. Ⓐ Ⓑ Ⓒ Ⓓ
14B. Ⓐ Ⓑ Ⓒ Ⓓ
15. Ⓐ Ⓑ Ⓒ Ⓓ
16. Ⓐ Ⓑ Ⓒ Ⓓ
17. Ⓐ Ⓑ Ⓒ Ⓓ
18. Ⓐ Ⓑ Ⓒ Ⓓ
19. Ⓐ Ⓑ Ⓒ Ⓓ
20A. Ⓐ Ⓑ Ⓒ Ⓓ
20B. Ⓐ Ⓑ Ⓒ Ⓓ
21. Ⓐ Ⓑ Ⓒ Ⓓ
22. //////////////////////
23. //////////////////////
24. Ⓐ Ⓑ Ⓒ Ⓓ
25. Ⓐ Ⓑ Ⓒ Ⓓ
26. Ⓐ Ⓑ Ⓒ Ⓓ
27. Ⓐ Ⓑ Ⓒ Ⓓ
28. //////////////////////

Copyright © by William H. Sadlier, Inc. All rights reserved.

Notes

Copyright © by William H. Sadlier, Inc. All rights reserved.

Name ____________________

Benchmark 3

1. (A) (B) (C) (D)
2A. (A) (B) (C) (D)
2B. (A) (B) (C) (D)
3A. (A) (B) (C) (D)
3B. (A) (B) (C) (D)
4A. (A) (B) (C) (D)
4B. (A) (B) (C) (D)
5. (A) (B) (C) (D)
6A. (A) (B) (C) (D)
6B. (A) (B) (C) (D)
7. (A) (B) (C) (D)
8A. (A) (B) (C) (D)
8B. (A) (B) (C) (D)
9A. (A) (B) (C) (D)
9B. (A) (B) (C) (D)
10. (A) (B) (C) (D)
11A. (A) (B) (C) (D)
11B. (A) (B) (C) (D)
12. (A) (B) (C) (D)
13. (A) (B) (C) (D)
14A. (A) (B) (C) (D)
14B. (A) (B) (C) (D)
15. (A) (B) (C) (D)
16. (A) (B) (C) (D)
17. (A) (B) (C) (D)
18. (A) (B) (C) (D)
19. (A) (B) (C) (D)
20A. (A) (B) (C) (D)
20B. (A) (B) (C) (D)
21. (A) (B) (C) (D)
22.
23.
24. (A) (B) (C) (D)
25. (A) (B) (C) (D)
26. (A) (B) (C) (D)
27. (A) (B) (C) (D)
28.

Benchmark 4

1. (A) (B) (C) (D)
2A. (A) (B) (C) (D)
2B. (A) (B) (C) (D)
3A. (A) (B) (C) (D)
3B. (A) (B) (C) (D)
4A. (A) (B) (C) (D)
4B. (A) (B) (C) (D)
5. (A) (B) (C) (D)
6A. (A) (B) (C) (D)
6B. (A) (B) (C) (D)
7. (A) (B) (C) (D)
8A. (A) (B) (C) (D)
8B. (A) (B) (C) (D)
9A. (A) (B) (C) (D)
9B. (A) (B) (C) (D)
10. (A) (B) (C) (D)
11A. (A) (B) (C) (D)
11B. (A) (B) (C) (D)
12. (A) (B) (C) (D)
13. (A) (B) (C) (D)
14A. (A) (B) (C) (D)
14B. (A) (B) (C) (D)
15. (A) (B) (C) (D)
16. (A) (B) (C) (D)
17. (A) (B) (C) (D)
18. (A) (B) (C) (D)
19. (A) (B) (C) (D)
20A. (A) (B) (C) (D)
20B. (A) (B) (C) (D)
21. (A) (B) (C) (D)
22.
23.
24. (A) (B) (C) (D)
25. (A) (B) (C) (D)
26. (A) (B) (C) (D)
27. (A) (B) (C) (D)
28.

Copyright © by William H. Sadlier, Inc. All rights reserved.

Notes

Copyright © by William H. Sadlier, Inc. All rights reserved.

Notes

Copyright © by William H. Sadlier, Inc. All rights reserved.